JOHN MARSHALL'S
DEFENSE OF
McCulloch v. Maryland

JOHN MARSHALL'S
DEFENSE OF
McCulloch v. Maryland

EDITED AND WITH AN INTRODUCTION BY
GERALD GUNTHER

STANFORD UNIVERSITY PRESS

STANFORD CALIFORNIA

1969

Stanford University Press
Stanford, California
© 1969 by the Board of Trustees of the
Leland Stanford Junior University
Printed in the United States of America
L.C. 70-93494
Cloth SBN 8047-0698-0
Paper SBN 8047-0699-9

Preface

I have sought to preserve the flavor of the 1819 debate, and I have therefore made no attempt to modernize style in editing these materials. Only outright errors and typographical curiosities have been eliminated—even though some of the stylistic inconsistencies that remain are no doubt attributable to the original printers rather than the authors. I have modified punctuation only where necessary to make meaning clear. The ellipses in the Hampden essays appeared in the newspaper; I have omitted nothing. My introductory essay avoids the usual academic regalia of reference notes. The most relevant citations are collected in my earlier essay, 21 *Stanford Law Review* 449 (1969).

This book is an outgrowth of my work on a volume of the History of the United States Supreme Court now in preparation under the auspices of the Permanent Committee for the Oliver Wendell Holmes Devise. I am grateful to the members of the Committee for permitting me to present here some of the findings I reported more briefly in the recent *Stanford Law Review* essay. Jean Allaway of the Library of Congress was helpful in producing photocopies from the Washington collections to confirm the hunches about location and attribution that I first pieced together while puzzling over my files in London. The New-York Historical Society gave permission to publish the substantial portion of John Marshall's letter of June 17, 1819, to Bushrod Washington. Fredericka Paff and Thomas J. Reilly of the *Stan-*

ford Law Review were especially helpful in the reprinting of the *Gazette* essays there. The plan for this fuller publication of the 1819 exchange was conceived in the fertile imaginations of Leon Seltzer and J. G. Bell of the Stanford University Press; I am grateful for their suggestion. Most of the burdensome editorial chores in preparing these essays for publication were undertaken, with efficiency and imaginativeness, by Betty K. Smith of the Stanford University Press. And, once again, I have reason to be grateful for Bess Hitchcock's devoted secretarial assistance.

G. G.

Contents

JOHN MARSHALL'S
DEFENSE OF
McCulloch v. Maryland

Introduction

An extraordinary debate is gathered in these pages: the great case of *McCulloch v. Maryland* and the cross fire of pseudonymous essays it provoked, with the Chief Justice of the United States in the unique role of waging newspaper battle with the chief ideological opponents of the Supreme Court. John Marshall delivered his nationalistic decision on March 6, 1819. Before the end of March, the *Richmond Enquirer*, the preeminent keeper of the states' rights flame, began publishing the first series of attacks—two essays signed "Amphictyon" and probably written by Judge William Brockenbrough. To Marshall, these seemed a major threat and one not likely to be countered by anyone else. And so the Chief Justice took pen in hand to defend himself and his Court and his principles: his reply to Amphictyon, over the signature "A Friend to the Union," appeared in the Philadelphia *Union* late in April. A few weeks later, the *Richmond Enquirer* printed an even more formidable challenge—four essays signed "Hampden" and written by the most energetic states' rights ideologue of all, Judge Spencer Roane of the Virginia Court of Appeals. Once again, Marshall was stirred into action: in late June 1819, he prepared a nine-part reply to Hampden, published in the Alexandria *Gazette* under the pseudonym "A Friend of the Constitution."

The remarkable exchange collected here contains much that is new. Before now, John Marshall was assumed to have written only one set of essays, not two; Spencer Roane was thought to be

Amphictyon as well as Hampden; Marshall's "Friend of the Constitution" pieces were entirely unknown; and his "Friend to the Union" essays were known only in garbled form. The allocation of power between nation and state is the pervasive problem of our federalism, *McCulloch* the most important case addressing that problem, Chief Justice Marshall's the most influential analysis. The appearance of fresh materials on this subject by these authors is extraordinary enough. But these essays are remarkable in content as well as novelty.

The most striking feature of the debate may well be the foresight of the essayists. They wrote about *McCulloch* at a time when many cared not about the case at all and most who cared were concerned only with its immediate result. There were only a very few, preeminently the prescient debaters on these pages, who had the long view, who cared deeply about the problems that have given *McCulloch* its pervasive significance. The newspaper exchange plainly reveals deep emotions and yet deals mainly in abstractions. In the 1819 context, it was unusual to emphasize general principles and display deep feelings in responding to *McCulloch*. To most, what was at issue in the case was no abstraction but a very concrete institution, the Second Bank of the United States. And what was decided was neither so surprising nor so central to the fate of the Bank to evoke intense reactions. Yet these intensely engaged essayists barely mention the Bank, hardly disagree about the immediate result. Their responses, which seemed so idiosyncratic, have proved to be the most perceptive ones. The emotionalism was not only genuine but justified. Roane and Brockenbrough and Marshall were aroused because there was indeed much at stake. And to battle over abstractions rather than immediate result was after all to fight over what really mattered: the continuingly relevant consequences inherent in the Court's premises and reasoning.

I

McCulloch v. Maryland was, most immediately though not most importantly, "the Bank Case." James McCulloch, Cashier of the Baltimore branch of the Second Bank of the United States, resisted Maryland's claim to a $15,000 tax on the Bank's operations. That dispute gave rise to the immediate questions before the Court. Had Congress acted within its constitutional powers in establishing the Bank in 1816? If so, could Maryland constitutionally tax the activities of the federally chartered institution? The Court held that the tax could not be collected: the federal incorporation was constitutional, the state tax unconstitutional.

It was a useful victory for the Bank, but hardly a decisive or even a surprising one. The decision came when the Bank had moved to the center of the nation's economic life and was well on its way to becoming a focus of political controversy as well. A severe postwar depression had developed in the months preceding the decision. Those hardest hit had found a highly visible, tempting target in the Bank, that economic colossus in which the government had only a minority interest, that nationwide commercial bank whose loans constituted the major source of credit and whose notes provided the major medium of exchange. State after state imposed hostile taxes on branches of the Bank. Criticism was voiced in Congress as well, and early in 1819 a special committee began investigating charges of oppression and mismanagement.

For the beleaguered Bank supporters, the Court victory meant a welcome boost to morale, but little more. Restoration of economic health, of Bank and nation, depended on forces more potent than the Court. And the Court's ruling was not necessary to counter the political threat from Congress—that had been averted before the Court decided. Moves to revoke the Bank's charter reached a climax in the House of Representatives in late February 1819, just as the Supreme Court began listening to the unusually long arguments of an unusually large group of lawyers in the *McCulloch* case. Congress rejected severe action against the Bank and adjourned on March 3, 1819—the very day effusive Baltimore lawyer William Pinkney concluded his argument for the Bank with an appeal to the Justices to "save the nation" and three days before John Marshall announced the unanimous ruling of the Court. Only in providing a shield from state taxes did the decision offer immediate aid to the Bank; and it took another battle, with Ohio, and another decision, five years later, to make that protection secure. "The Bank Case" would certainly not be "the Great Case" had it produced no more than this marginally significant victory for the Bank.

Nor was the immediate constitutional holding of the case any more earthshaking than its economic and political impact. To assert in 1819 that Congress had the power to establish a national bank was to validate an existing consensus, not to break new ground. The constitutionality of a national bank had once been a major battleground in the clashes between broad and narrow interpretations of congressional powers. That issue had split the Cabinet in 1791, when President Washington asked for advice about the law chartering the First Bank. Secretary of the Treasury Alexander Hamilton had justified it at length. Secretary of State Thomas Jefferson had elaborately argued its unconstitutionality; and for years his position was a basic creed for Jeffersonian Republicans. Jeffersonian principles had blocked renewal of the charter of the First Bank in 1811, but they had eroded under the pressure of the economic difficulties Jefferson's successor encountered during the War of 1812. By 1815 President Madison was prepared to suppress his constitutional doubts. And in 1816 most Jeffersonian Republicans supported the incorporation of the Second Bank. Though popular support of the Bank had waned by 1819, the 1816 constitutional consensus had not been substantially impaired. The attacks aired in Congress while *McCulloch* was before the Court were directed mainly at operations, not constitutionality.

The old constitutional arguments reemerged in the Supreme Court argument in *McCulloch*, to be sure. But even the lawyers who advocated them at greatest length were apologetic about repeating contentions made "threadbare" by frequent reiteration of Hamilton's and Jefferson's positions. The holding that the 1816 law was valid was wholly unsurprising: no one expected the Marshall Court to embrace Jefferson's tenets after even Jefferson's party had abandoned them. That holding merely added the Court's imprimatur to a widespread agreement about the constitutionality of the Bank. Only the constitutionality of a state tax on a validly established national organ was at all a doubtful question in the case.

Yet *McCulloch*'s greatness lay precisely in its justification of the most expectable part of its conclusion. *McCulloch* illustrates what many given to cheering or condemning the Supreme Court forget: that with the Court, because it is a court, lasting impact ultimately turns on the persuasiveness of the reasons it articulates, not on the particular result it reaches. It was appreciation of that basic source of judicial strength that spurred Marshall and the *Enquirer* essayists. It was Marshall's principles that troubled Brockenbrough and Roane, the Chief Justice knew; it was to thwart the future impact of those principles that the Amphictyon and Hampden essays were published.

To conclude that the Bank was constitutional was to beat a moribund horse. But to explain that the Bank was constitutional because the Constitution should be broadly and flexibly interpreted, because one could not expect such a document to specify every power that the national government might properly exert, because one should not be miserly in finding implied national powers, because Congress legitimately had broad discretion in

selecting means to achieve the ends listed in the recital of delegated national powers in the Constitution—all this was to touch
a very live nerve indeed. With his elaborate endorsement of constitutional flexibility and congressional discretion, Marshall un-
mistakably cast the Court's weight on the centralizing side in the
recurrent struggle about allocation of authority between nation
and states. With this opinion, the Court provided a reservoir of
justifications for national action perhaps even fuller than Marshall intended—one repeatedly drawn on during the Era of Good
Feelings and the Age of the Robber Barons and the New Deal
and our civil rights crises by those who have sought to expand the
area of national competence.

But the opinion was more than a contribution to debates to
come. It was a message with immediate relevance as well, to rally
the sagging forces of nationalism and to combat the mounting
constitutional self-doubts in Congress. The 1819 consensus regarding the desirability and legitimacy of a national bank did not
carry over to other national programs. The adoption of the 1816
bank law came at a time of euphoric nationalism fed by postwar
patriotic pride and economic boom. That atmosphere yielded vi-
sions of a range of other national institutions, from a national university to a strengthened peacetime military establishment and,
most important of all, a nationwide system of internal improvements, of roads and canals. Even in 1816, however, the stilling of
old constitutional doubts was not pervasive enough to assure support for all national projects. President Madison acquiesced in
the heresy of a bank but insisted that only a constitutional amendment could authorize a national system of roads and canals. Congress nonetheless enacted an internal improvements bill, which
was ultimately vetoed by Madison.

By 1818, however, the buoyant postwar nationalism had been
considerably deflated. James Monroe, the new President, was
nearly as much of a constitutional skeptic about internal improvements as Madison, as his first State of the Union message made

clear. And, perhaps more significantly, it soon became apparent that the supporters of the constitutionality of federal internal improvements were no longer in the majority in Congress. In a debate especially relevant to *McCulloch*, a debate that began precisely one year before the date of that decision, Speaker Henry Clay asked the House to support internal improvements as appropriate means to implement the congressional powers regarding commerce, post roads, and war. Clay's two lengthy speeches, in passage after striking passage, abound with close parallels to the arguments set forth by Marshall a year later. The House had an opportunity to respond to Clay's appeal by voting on a number of resolutions, each of which invoked a different constitutionally delegated power as the source of an implied national power to build roads and canals. The response demonstrated that congressional sentiment had changed since 1816: each resolution fell short of majority support.

Congress's mounting constitutional doubts about proposed national programs may be the most significant ingredients of the *McCulloch* context. With respect to the Bank, the *McCulloch* decision offered a peripheral blessing to a continuing consensus. With respect to the ongoing debate, the Court's rationale gave impetus, not mere approval. Clay's failure to muster support for the resolutions was a reminder that the 1816 acceptance of a national bank signified not the end of strict construction of the Constitution but rather a shifting of the battle to other fronts. Roads and canals had become the most prominent one; in later times it would be tariffs and slavery and trust-busting, and labor relations, and poverty programs, and voting rights.

The major thrust of *McCulloch* is obvious with the perspective of 150 years; but in 1819 the newspaper debaters were among the few perceptive ones. The essays say little about the Bank. Amphictyon, especially, reveals anxiety about the implications of the *McCulloch* rationale for internal improvements. But predominant throughout the debate is the focus on the abstractions, on consolidation and states' rights, on implied powers and appropriate means—the abstractions decisive in the development of American federalism.

And yet, though *McCulloch* is the great case because it was a roads and canals case and especially an implied powers case, its Bank case aspects remain inextricable. The Bank question was the only major controversy about congressional powers to come before the Marshall Court. The Court can speak only in an actual lawsuit before it; without the *McCulloch* controversy, there would have been no legitimate occasion to make statements with such obvious relevance to internal improvements and tariffs and slavery. But the inseparable Bank context of those statements could only be an albatross for the nationalist cause generally. The Bank was an unpopular institution. The specific parties carrying the Bank banner, McCulloch and his associates at the Baltimore branch, were suspected of being wild speculators just before the decision and were discovered to be outrageous embezzlers soon after. Inevitably, some of the criticism of the decision focused on these easy targets. But the newspaper debaters adhered steadfastly to the longer view: what moved Brockenbrough and Roane to challenge and Marshall to explain and defend were more basic, more continuingly relevant concerns.

II

Even some of John Marshall's friends thought him hypersensitive about the pieces in the *Richmond Enquirer*. Yet there was reason enough for anxiety in their appearance in that particular paper. The *Enquirer* was not just another local newspaper. It was the organ of the Richmond Junto, one of the nation's most effective political leadership groups. Newspapers throughout the country frequently reprinted materials that the *Enquirer*'s energetic editor, Thomas Ritchie, chose to put into its pages. And the untiring interest in the paper shown by Ritchie's cousin, Spencer

Roane, rested on more than family ties: Roane not only was the most prominent judge on the highest Virginia court, but also led the Junto political machine.

The Junto had a more disciplined following when it came to filling offices, from county judge to governor, than when unswerving loyalty to states' rights ideology was at issue. Yet even abstract discourses were likely to carry more weight for coming from a source known for success in political practice, not merely skill in theory. Indeed, Marshall's apprehension was justifiably greater just because theory predominated in the *Enquirer* essays, just because Amphictyon and Hampden eschewed the usual and easy route of rallying loud but merely temporary hostility to the Court from those injured by the immediate result. Virginia was not one of the states seeking to tax the Bank out of existence. The Junto leaders were not vehement Bank enemies; many, indeed, had close economic and personal ties with the Bank's Richmond branch. The critics' inattention to the pro-Bank result might make the immediate threat less than Marshal feared, but their preoccupation with the implications of the reasoning justified his long-range concern: it showed that they shared his sense of what was ephemeral and what was truly important about *McCulloch*.

That the most intense criticism should emanate from Virginia was additional reason for Marshall to be apprehensive. His home state was the ideological seedbed of states' rights. Though quiescent in recent years, it was now apparently getting ready to resume its dominant role. Virginia's anti-Federalists—including Patrick Henry, Spencer Roane's father-in-law—had led the fight against John Marshall and his fellow supporters of the Constitution in the ratification debates of the 1780's. Virginia's Resolutions of 1798 and Madison's Committee Report of 1799, attacking the Alien and Sedition Acts as beyond congressional competence, had elaborated the case against broad construction and had asserted the state's obligation to interpose itself against excessive national authority. After the Jeffersonians attained power at the turn of the century, the responsibilities of office exerted pressure toward nationalism and tempered the strict constructionist faith.

Yet a strain of unreconstructed Republicanism had always persisted, even while most followers of Jefferson and Madison abandoned many constitutional scruples. John Randolph of Roanoke and John Taylor of Caroline personified that orthodox heritage. And Spencer Roane and the *Richmond Enquirer* were its most articulate spokesmen. They did indeed support Madison against the states' rights attacks of New England Federalists who found the Principles of '98 an increasingly useful weapon against the hated War of 1812. But even then, when most old Republicans and most old Federalists managed to execute an ideological about-face, Spencer Roane had refused to totally abandon the old creed. In 1814, in his official capacity on the highest state court, he concluded that the United States Supreme Court could not constitutionally review state court decisions on questions of federal law. Roane's loyalty to the Republicans in Washington was strong enough to postpone the publication of the decision in *Hunter v. Martin* for a year, to avoid giving undue aid and comfort to the New England secessionists planning the Hartford Convention. But his adherence to the old principles was too strong to repress for long, even while most Republicans were at the zenith of their nationalism.

Given this background, the *Enquirer* encores of Virginia's siren song of states' rights carried especially ominous overtones for one listener, John Marshall. Echoes of never wholly silenced melodies resound throughout the Amphictyon and the Hampden essays and Marshall's replies: the references to the *Federalist* papers and the ratification debates of the 1780's, to Madison's Report of 1799, to the Virginia court's defiance of the Supreme Court in 1815.

In the spring of 1819, the essays seemed antiquarian to many. Attacking the Court for its nationalistic principles, with ideology the genuine target rather than merely a makeweight, appeared quixotic. But to a few, to Marshall and Roane especially, the principles of constitutional interpretation were what really mattered. In the spring of 1819, Roane and Marshall each believed that his was a lone voice in the wilderness. But those with consistent positions on national power and states' rights would gain allies from the ranks of the more result-oriented as circumstances changed. In the spring of 1819, Amphictyon and Hampden found few supporters, even in Richmond. But as the economic crisis grew, more receptive audiences would develop among those ready to identify financial distress with the rise of national institutions. And by the end of the year, when the debate about the admission of Missouri brought slavery to the fore as an additional stimulus, even broader support for attacks on expansive claims of national authority would come forth.

With respect to immediate risk to the Court and the Union, Marshall's assessment of the attacks on *McCulloch* was indeed exaggerated. But his sense of the significance of the ideological controversy was vindicated even in relatively short-range terms, by the support for states' rights that mounted in the following months. And the reverberations of the 1819 debaters' ideas in all the many subsequent disputes about the scope of national powers leave no doubt that Marshall's concern with defending *McCulloch* rested on a sound long-range judgment.

III

In mid-March 1819, one week after the decision in *McCulloch v. Maryland*, the Supreme Court adjourned. John Marshall returned to his Richmond home. Almost immediately, he learned that a newspaper attack was in the making: Richmond's social circles were not so large or so ideologically divided as to keep the Republican Junto's political gossip from the Federalist Chief Justice's ears. "Our opinion in the Bank has roused the sleeping

spirit of Virginia—if indeed it ever sleeps," he wrote his colleague
from Massachusetts, Joseph Story. Justice Story was as nationalistic as the Chief Justice, although he owed his appointment to
James Madison: Story's Republicanism evolved from the confident centralizing strains of Jeffersonianism in power, not from
the suspicious localist Jeffersonianism of 1798. And Story was by
no means unaware of the persistence of states' rights views in Virginia: he had spoken for the Supreme Court in *Martin v. Hunter's Lessee* in 1816, which squelched the challenge to appellate
jurisdiction from Roane's court. But in the North, Marshall's
warning that the decision would soon be attacked "with asperity,"
a warning conveyed to Court Reporter Henry Wheaton as well
as to Story, seemed less threatening. The Chief Justice displayed
an "unusual degree of solicitude," Wheaton wrote; there was
after all no immediate likelihood that Virginians would find any
other state "to join them in their crusade against the federal
authority."

    In Richmond, the risks seemed greater, especially if the attacks
went unanswered. Marshall was haunted by the prospect of a
one-sided barrage of criticisms, for Court supporters "never write
for the publick." It was to Justice Bushrod Washington, who had
gone North to attend to lower court duties in Philadelphia, that
the Chief Justice poured out his worries at greatest length. Washington was likley to be the most understanding listener, for there
were ties binding Marshall more closely to him than to any other
associate. Both were Virginia Federalists; they had shared nearly two decades on the Court; and it was Washington, the nephew
of George Washington and the executor of his estate, who had
induced Marshall to write his lengthy biography of the first
President. "We shall be denounced bitterly in the papers," Marshall wrote Washington, "& as not a word will be said on the
other side we shall undoubtedly be condemned as a pack of con-
solidating aristocratics." The "politicians of Virginia" were voic-

ing "great dissatisfaction" with *McCulloch*, and not because of the pro-Bank result; indeed, the Virginians "would probably have been seriously offended with us had we dared to have decided otherwise." What they objected to, it was plain to Marshall, was the rationale behind the assertion of national and judicial authority. What they wanted was "an obsequious, silent opinion without reasons"—not the specific holding, "but our heretical reasoning is pronounced most damnable." The Bank law was the responsibility of President and Congress, but they "have power & places to bestow" and will therefore "escape with impunity." It was "the poor court who have nothing to give & of whom nobody is afraid" that would be the sole target.

Three days later, on March 30, 1819, the first Amphictyon attack, precisely along the lines anticipated by Marshall, appeared in the *Enquirer*. Historians have erroneously ascribed the Amphictyon pieces, like the longer and more acerbic Hampden ones published ten weeks later, to Spencer Roane. That attribution is wrong: Amphictyon was another member of the Richmond Junto, probably Judge William Brockenbrough, as John Marshall himself believed. But that did not make it any less an authentic challenge by the "politicians of Virginia": Brockenbrough was a friend of Ritchie and an acquaintance of Roane, and an orthodox Jeffersonian, opposed to extending the authority of federal courts and troubled by any sign of expanding power in the national government—even in the executive branch, which was still in Virginia Republican hands.

John Marshall found the Amphictyon essays impossible to bear in silence. If they went unchallenged, their surface plausibility would help spread the states' rights virus throughout the land. The Chief Justice was sufficiently concerned about proprieties to conceal his identity, but not enough to abstain from writing. Fortunately, Brother Washington was still in Philadelphia to place Marshall's replies in the Federalist paper there.

And so, a month after the Amphictyon essays appeared, the Philadelphia *Union* printed John Marshall's response over the nom de plume "A Friend to the Union."

Historians have found the essays that appeared in the *Union* murky and tortured. That is not surprising: what the *Union* printed was not what Marshall wrote. The Philadelphia printer, as Marshall complained to Washington, had produced "a curious piece of work": "He has cut out the middle of the first number to be inserted into the middle of the second; & to show his perfect impartiality, has cut out the middle of the second number to be inserted in the first. He has thrown these disrupted parts together without the least regard to their fitness." In that Philadelphia version, Marshall's reasoning looks indeed like "a labyrinth," an offering "nauseous to the intellectual palate." And that "mangled" version has been the basis for historical judgments down to the present day.

In this book the essays of "A Friend to the Union" are for the first time readily available in their intended and intelligible sequence. Marshall himself provided the instructions for untangling the Philadelphia morass; he specified the proper form in telling Washington of his wish that his answer "should appear in its true shape" in Virginia. And Washington, now back home at Mount Vernon, found a nearby outlet: there is a heretofore unknown, correct republication of "A Friend to the Union" in issues of the Alexandria *Gazette* in mid-May 1819.

But the received historical view of the *Union* essays is in error in a more basic respect. It has been assumed that the unsatisfactory *Union* experience marked the end of Marshall's journalistic efforts. Marshall's letters show that he wrote responses to the *Enquirer*'s later Hampden pieces, but inattention to dates led earlier commentators to the chronologically untenable belief that the Philadelphia *Union* essays constituted that response. A more careful search in light of the leads supplied by Marshall's correspondence has now unearthed the true response to Hampden,

Marshall's only answer to Spencer Roane, the nine essays by "A Friend of the Constitution" in the Alexandria *Gazette*.

Contrary to the traditional view, Marshall did not withdraw from the newspaper battle after his frustrating experience with the Philadelphia *Union*. The attack was too intense, the stakes too important, to permit disgust with the *Union*'s "curious mixture" to turn into paralysis. The Philadelphia garble did indeed lead him to squelch Story's interest in seeking Northern republication of the essays. But he was not giving up the struggle, only shifting his focus. His second major newspaper foray would be in the Alexandria *Gazette*. This time, the enemy was Spencer Roane himself. This time, the forum was his home environment, not the North. This time, the chief target was the Virginia legislature, not general public opinion.

A week after his *Union* essays appeared, Marshall told Washington that his fears were greater than ever. The Virginia states' righters were likely to intensify their agitation. A "very serious" attack on the Court in the next session of the legislature, at the end of the year, would "undoubtedly" be made. There would be efforts "to pass resolutions not very unlike those which were called forth by the alien & sedition laws of 1799." And, more immediately, there were rumors "that some other essays, written by a very great man, are now preparing & will soon appear." "The democracy in Virginia," Marshall reported to Story soon after, would continue to denounce *McCulloch* through the usual techniques: "To excite this ferment the opinion has been grossly misrepresented; and where its argument has been truly stated it has been met by principles too palpably absurd for intelligent men. But prejudice will swallow anything." If these principles prevailed, he feared, "the constitution would be converted into the old confederation."

The anxiety about additional essays was well-founded. The "very great man," as Marshall knew, was his arch-rival, Spencer Roane. And the first of Roane's four Hampden essays began to appear in the *Enquirer* within weeks. Before the Hampden series had run its course, Marshall resolved to take up the pen once more, so that the Junto leader's fulminations would not prevail by default when the legislature convened. The mood and motivation underlying these newly discovered Alexandria *Gazette* essays are best captured in another letter from Marshall to Washington, written on June 17, 1819, two days after the second Hampden essay was published:

The storm which has been for some time threatening the Judges has at length burst on their heads & a most furious hurricane it is. The author is spoken of with as much confidence as if his name was subscribed to his essays. It is worth your while to read them. They are in the Enquirer under the signature of Hampden.

I find myself more stimulated on this subject than on any other because I believe the design to be to injure the Judges & impair the constitution. I have therefore thoughts of answering these essays & sending my pieces to you for publication in the Alexandria paper. I shall send them on in successive numbers but do not wish the first to be published till I shall have seen the last of Hampden. I will then write to you & request you to have the publications made immediately. As the numbers will be marked I hope no mistake will be made by the printer & that the manuscript will be given to the flames. I wish two papers of each number to be directed to T. Marshall, Oak Hill, Fauquier. I do not wish them to come to me lest some suspicion of the author should be created.

During those late June days, Marshall worked with mounting intensity on his ever-expanding reply to Hampden. At first, three numbers seemed adequate. Then, he planned two others. Ultimately, the series ran to four more—nine in all. Indications that Hampden, like Amphictyon, had created less of a stir in Richmond than Marshall had originally feared did not diminish the Chief Justice's zeal. It was now plain that the *Enquirer* essays were really "designed for the country & have had considerable influence there." And it was that influence that might be translatable into immediate political consequences when the legislature convened: "I wish the refutation to be in the hands of some respectable members of the legislature so it may prevent some act of the assembly [both] silly & wicked."

Occasionally, Marshall continued to show concern about concealing his identity. At one point, he suggested changing the *Gazette* pseudonym to "A Constitutionalist": "A Friend of the Constitution is so much like a Friend of the Union that it may lead to some suspicion of identity." But that was plainly a secondary matter "of no great consequence": the overriding aim was to defend *McCulloch* against the threatened Junto attack. That attack reached its height in February 1820, when the lower house of the Virginia legislature adopted anti-Court, anti-*McCulloch* resolutions. But the challenge stalled there. The state's attention was distracted by the Missouri Compromise dispute, though Roane continued to focus on his main target, the Marshall Court, with his vitriolic essays on *Cohens v. Virginia* in 1821. But John Marshall had taken to the newspapers for the last time in 1819. Henceforth he would confine his public proclamations of friendship for the Constitution to the pages of the Court's official reports.

IV

For a more discreet Chief Justice, those official reports would have been the sole outlet for constitutional exegesis in 1819 as well. But had Marshall used greater restraint, we would have been deprived of the remarkable opportunity, through materials that have come to the surface after a century and a half, to hear the most important figure in Supreme Court history speak about the most important issue before his Court. That opportunity would be valuable even if the *Union* and *Gazette* essays did no more than restate the known. But essays so intense and so wide-ranging are bound to enrich our understanding, of man and of issue.

John Marshall, these essays confirm, had a passionate personal commitment to the principles of *McCulloch*. And the production of essays of such vigor and length and complexity at such speed should help lay to rest some doubts occasionally raised about the extent of Marshall's contribution to his Court. Could he really be responsible for so large a proportion of the Court's output? Surely the length of these newspaper pieces makes an affirmative answer more credible. Could Marshall really have produced the *McCulloch* opinion in the brief three days between the close of argument and the date of decision—while listening to submissions in other cases for several hours each day? Is it not more likely that, confident about what he wanted to say, he had his drafts ready weeks or months before the Court Term? The timing of his replies to Amphictyon and Hampden corroborates the conclusion that *McCulloch* was indeed written in response to the week-and-a-half-long argument, not in advance. Was the elaboration of general principles Marshall's sole strength? Was he uninterested in or incompetent on the details of formal learning? Did he have to rely on more scholarly colleagues like Story for the legalistic trim? Those conjectures, too, are refuted here. Sitting alone in Richmond, deeply stirred because the principles dearest to him seemed at stake, Marshall took on Brockenbrough and Roane on the level of technical detail as well as of general philosophy. With great care, point by point—indeed, too tediously for polemic effectiveness—he replied to the state judges' invocations of common law and international law and engaged them toe to toe on the true meaning of the learned treatise writers, of Vattel and Grotius and Lord Coke.

But the real richness of these essays ultimately lies in the realm of ideas, in their irresistible invitation to speculate anew about the primary issue: how far-reaching is the range of congressional discretion legitimated by *McCulloch v. Maryland*? The major charge by Roane and Brockenbrough was that *McCulloch's* principles endorsed a virtually unlimited central authority, that the

Court had set forth no viable limits on national power. And the thrust of Marshall's response was to deny that charge of consolidation, to insist, with more emphasis than in *McCulloch* itself, that those principles did not give Congress carte blanche, that they did preserve a true federal system in which the central government was limited in its powers—and that the limits were capable of judicial enforcement.

The perspective of a century and a half shows that many of the fears voiced in the *Richmond Enquirer* have indeed been borne out. Political restraints, not constitutional principles in the Court's keeping, impose what federalism limits remain on congressional authority. As Congress has expanded into areas formerly in the state domain, the centralizing process has typically taken place in the name of *McCulloch v. Maryland*. When the Court sustained the labor laws and farm controls and factory standards of the New Deal, *McCulloch* was invoked. More recently, the Court's validation of the Voting Rights Act of 1965 and the public accommodations provisions of the 1964 Civil Rights Act prominently featured excerpts from Marshall's language in *McCulloch*.

What, then, does one make of Marshall's emphatic assurances here that substantial, judicially enforceable limitations on congressional power existed? That is the main question inherent in this collection, and it is not easily answered. One conceivable approach to an answer is to view the centralizing progeny of *Mc-Culloch* as offspring fully contemplated by Marshall and accordingly to dismiss the *Union* and *Gazette* essays as clever defensive propaganda designed to induce disbelief of the *Enquirer* charges that the emperor wore no clothes. I find a different approach persuasive. I am not convinced that the modern, most expansive reading of *McCulloch* is the inevitable one. I do not believe that the moderate interpretation suggested by these essays should be discounted.

I would suggest, rather, that the *Union* and *Gazette* pieces form, with the *McCulloch* opinion itself, parts of a coherent whole. For me, Marshall's newspaper commentary reflects genuine views, not disingenuous facade. Marshall claimed to be outraged by Roane's charges that *McCulloch* had given "a general letter of attorney to the future legislators of the union," that the Court "had resolved to put down all discussions respecting the powers of the government in the future," that the decision "granted to congress unlimited powers under the pretext of a discretion in selecting means." I believe that Marshall's outrage was real. His essays and their context indicate that he did not view *McCulloch* as embracing extreme nationalism. The degree of centralization that has taken place since his time may well have come about in the face of Marshall's intent rather than in accord with his expectations. That centralization may be the inevitable consequence of economic and social changes. And this development may suggest the impossibility of articulating general constitutional standards capable of limiting those centralizing forces, particularly through judicial action.

But to say this is very different from saying that Marshall knew he was engaging in a hopeless task, or indeed that he wanted to see the prophecies of consolidation fulfilled. His essays indicate, rather, that he did not believe that Congress had an unrestricted choice of means to accomplish delegated ends. He opposed extreme formulations, excessively broad as well as unduly narrow, of the range of legitimate means—"neither a feigned convenience nor a strict necessity; but a reasonable convenience, and a qualified necessity" was a guide he endorsed in the *Gazette*. Moreover, these pieces suggest that Marshall was quite serious in his often neglected assurance in *McCulloch*, reiterated and elaborated in the *Gazette*, that the Court would hold an act unconstitutional should Congress, "under the pretext of executing its powers, pass laws for the accomplishment of objects, not entrusted to the government." Clearly these essays give cause to be more guarded in invoking *McCulloch* to support views of congressional power now thought necessary. If virtually unlimited congressional discretion is indeed required to meet twentieth-century needs, candid argument to that effect, rather than ritual invoking of Marshall's authority, would seem to me more closely in accord with the Chief Justice's stance.

These impressions are open to challenge. What is beyond doubt is that the debate collected here demands speculation about these issues. We cannot avoid coming to terms with Marshall's commentary so long as we seek new solutions to the perennial problems of federal-state relationships. And especially so long as we look to *McCulloch v. Maryland* as the fountainhead of national powers, concern with these newly available Marshall elaborations is a civic obligation as well as an irresistible temptation.

Marshall's Opinion in *McCulloch v. Maryland*

4 Wheaton's Reports 400 (March 6, 1819)

Mr. Chief Justice MARSHALL delivered the opinion of the Court. In the case now to be determined, the defendant, a sovereign State, denies the obligation of a law enacted by the legislature of the Union, and the plaintiff, on his part, contests the validity of an act which has been passed by the legislature of that State. The constitution of our country, in its most interesting and vital parts, is to be considered; the conflicting powers of the government of the Union and of its members, as marked in that constitution, are to be discussed; and an opinion given, which may essentially influence the great operations of the government. No tribunal can approach such a question without a deep sense of its importance, and of the awful responsibility involved in its decision. But it must be decided peacefully, or remain a source of hostile legislation, perhaps of hostility of a still more serious nature; and if it is to be so decided, by this tribunal alone can the decision be made. On the Supreme Court of the United States has the constitution of our country devolved this important duty.

The first question made in the cause is, has Congress power to incorporate a bank?

It has been truly said, that this can scarcely be considered as an open question, entirely unprejudiced by the former proceedings of the nation respecting it. The principle now contested was introduced at a very early period of our history, has been recognized by many successive legislatures, and has been acted upon by the judicial department, in cases of peculiar delicacy, as a law of undoubted obligation.

It will not be denied, that a bold and daring usurpation might be resisted, after an acquiescence still longer and more complete than this. But it is conceived that a doubtful question, one on which human reason may pause, and the human judgment be suspended, in the decision of which the great principles of liberty are not concerned, but the respective powers of those who are equally the representatives of the people, are to be adjusted; if not put at rest by the practice of the government, ought to receive a considerable impression from that practice. An exposition of the constitution, deliberately established by legislative acts, on the faith of which an immense property has been advanced, ought not to be lightly disregarded.

The power now contested was exercised by the first Congress elected under the present constitution. The bill for incorporating the bank of the United States did not steal upon an unsuspecting legislature, and pass unobserved. Its principle was completely understood, and was opposed with equal zeal and ability. After being resisted, first in the fair and open field of debate, and afterwards in the executive cabinet, with as much persevering talent as any measure has ever experienced, and being supported by arguments which convinced minds as pure and as intelligent as this country can boast, it became a law. The original act was permitted to expire; but a short experience of the embarrassments to which the refusal to revive it exposed the government, convinced those who were most prejudiced against the measure of its necessity, and induced the passage of the present law. It would require no ordinary share of intrepidity to assert that a measure adopted under these circumstances was a bold and plain usurpation, to which the constitution gave no countenance.

These observations belong to the cause; but they are not made under the impression that, were the question entirely new, the law would be found irreconcilable with the constitution.

In discussing this question, the counsel for the State of Maryland have deemed it of some importance, in the construction of the constitution, to consider that instrument not as emanating from the people, but as the act of sovereign and independent States. The powers of the general government, it has been said, are delegated by the States, who alone are truly sovereign; and must be exercised in subordination to the States, who alone possess supreme dominion.

It would be difficult to sustain this proposition. The Convention which framed the constitution was indeed elected by the State legislatures. But the instrument, when it came from their hands, was a mere proposal, without obligation, or pretensions to it. It was reported to the then existing Congress of the United States, with a request that it might "be submitted to a Convention of Delegates, chosen in each State by the people thereof, under the recommendation of its Legislature, for their assent and ratification." This mode of proceeding was adopted; and by the Convention, by Congress, and by the State Legislatures, the instrument was submitted to the people. They acted upon it in the only manner in which they can act safely, effectively, and wisely, on such a subject, by assembling in Convention. It is true, they assembled in their several States—and where else should they have assembled? No political dreamer was ever wild enough to think of breaking down the lines which separate the States, and of compounding the American people into one common mass. Of consequence, when they act, they act in their States. But the measures they adopt do not, on that account, cease to be the measures of the people themselves, or become the measures of the State governments.

From these Conventions the constitution derives its whole authority. The government proceeds directly from the people; is "ordained and established" in the name of the people; and is declared to be ordained, "in order to form a more perfect union, establish justice, ensure domestic tranquillity, and secure the blessings of liberty to themselves and to their posterity." The assent of the States, in their sovereign capacity, is implied in calling a

Convention, and thus submitting that instrument to the people. But the people were at perfect liberty to accept or reject it; and their act was final. It required not the affirmance, and could not be negatived, by the State governments. The constitution, when thus adopted, was of complete obligation, and bound the State sovereignties.

It has been said, that the people had already surrendered all their powers to the State sovereignties, and had nothing more to give, But, surely, the question whether they may resume and modify the powers granted to government does not remain to be settled in this country. Much more might the legitimacy of the general government be doubted, had it been created by the States. The powers delegated to the State sovereignties were to be exercised by themselves, not by a distinct and independent sovereignty, created by themselves. To the formation of a league, such as was the confederation, the State sovereignties were certainly competent. But when, "in order to form a more perfect union," it was deemed necessary to change this alliance into an effective government, possessing great and sovereign powers, and acting directly on the people, the necessity of referring it to the people, and of deriving its powers directly from them, was felt and acknowledged by all.

The government of the Union, then (whatever may be the influence of this fact on the case), is, emphatically, and truly, a government of the people. In form and in substance it emanates from them. Its powers are granted by them, and are to be exercised directly on them, and for their benefit.

This government is acknowledged by all to be one of enumerated powers. The principle, that it can exercise only the powers granted to it, would seem too apparent to have required to be enforced by all those arguments which its enlightened friends, while it was depending before the people, found it necessary to urge. That principle is now universally admitted. But the question respecting the extent of the powers actually granted, is perpetually arising, and will probably continue to arise, as long as our system shall exist.

In discussing these questions, the conflicting powers of the general and State governments must be brought into view, and the supremacy of their respective laws, when they are in opposition, must be settled.

If any one proposition could command the universal assent of mankind, we might expect it would be this—that the government of the Union, though limited in its powers, is supreme within its sphere of action. This would seem to result necessarily from its nature. It is the government of all; its powers are delegated by all; it represents all, and acts for all. Though any one State may be willing to control its operations, no State is willing to allow others to control them. The nation, on those subjects on which it can act, must necessarily bind its component parts. But this question is not left to mere reason: the people have, in express terms, decided it, by saying, "this constitution, and the laws of the United States, which shall be made in pursuance thereof," "shall be the supreme law of the land," and by requiring that the members of the State legislatures, and the officers of the executive and judicial departments of the States, shall take the oath of fidelity to it.

The government of the United States, then, though limited in its powers, is supreme; and its laws, when made in pursuance of the constitution, form the supreme law of the land, "any thing in the constitution or laws of any State to the contrary notwithstanding."

Among the enumerated powers, we do not find that of establishing a bank or creating a corporation. But there is no phrase in the instrument which, like the articles of confederation, excludes incidental or implied powers; and which requires that every thing granted shall be expressly and minutely described. Even the 10th amendment, which was framed for the purpose of quieting the excessive jealousies which had been excited, omits the word "expressly," and declares only that the powers "not delegated to the

United States, nor prohibited to the States, are reserved to the States or to the people;" thus leaving the question, whether the particular power which may become the subject of contest has been delegated to the one government, or prohibited to the other, to depend on a fair construction of the whole instrument. The men who drew and adopted this amendment had experienced the embarrassments resulting from the insertion of this word in the articles of confederation, and probably omitted it to avoid those embarrassments. A constitution, to contain an accurate detail of all the subdivisions of which its great powers will admit, and of all the means by which they may be carried into execution, would partake of the prolixity of a legal code, and could scarcely be embraced by the human mind. It would probably never be understood by the public. Its nature, therefore, requires, that only its great outlines should be marked, its important objects designated, and the minor ingredients which compose those objects be deduced from the nature of the objects themselves. That this idea was entertained by the framers of the American constitution, is not only to be inferred from the nature of the instrument, but from the language. Why else were some of the limitations, found in the ninth section of the 1st article, introduced? It is also, in some degree, warranted by their having omitted to use any restrictive term which might prevent its receiving a fair and just interpretation. In considering this question, then, we must never forget, that it is *a constitution* we are expounding.

Although, among the enumerated powers of government, we do not find the word "bank" or "incorporation," we find the great powers to lay and collect taxes; to borrow money; to regulate commerce; to declare and conduct a war; and to raise and support armies and navies. The sword and the purse, all the external relations, and no inconsiderable portion of the industry of the nation, are entrusted to its government. It can never be pretended that these vast powers draw after them others of inferior importance, merely because they are inferior. Such an idea can never be advanced. But it may with great reason be contended, that a government, entrusted with such ample powers, on the due execution of which the happiness and prosperity of the nation so vitally depends, must also be entrusted with ample means for their execution. The power being given, it is the interest of the nation to facilitate its execution. It can never be their interest, and cannot be presumed to have been their intention, to clog and embarrass its execution by withholding the most appropriate means. Throughout this vast republic, from the St. Croix to the Gulph of Mexico, from the Atlantic to the Pacific, revenue is to be collected and expended, armies are to be marched and supported. The exigencies of the nation may require that the treasure raised in the north should be transported to the south, *that* raised in the east conveyed to the west, or that this order should be reversed. Is that construction of the constitution to be preferred which would render these operations difficult, hazardous, and expensive? Can we adopt that construction (unless the words imperiously require it), which would impute to the framers of that instrument, when granting these powers for the public good, the intention of impeding their exercise by withholding a choice of means? If, indeed, such be the mandate of the constitution, we have only to obey; but that instrument does not profess to enumerate the means by which the powers it confers may be executed; nor does it prohibit the creation of a corporation, if the existence of such a being be essential to the beneficial exercise of those powers. It is, then, the subject of fair inquiry, how far such means may be employed.

It is not denied, that the powers given to the government imply the ordinary means of execution. That, for example, of raising revenue, and applying it to national purposes, is admitted to imply the power of conveying money from place to place, as the exigencies of the nation may require, and of employing the usual means of conveyance. But it is denied that the government has its choice of means; or, that it may employ the most convenient means, if, to employ them, it be necessary to erect a corporation.

On what foundation does this argument rest? On this alone:

The power of creating a corporation, is one appertaining to sovereignty, and is not expressly conferred on Congress. This is true. But all legislative powers appertain to sovereignty. The original power of giving the law on any subject whatever, is a sovereign power; and if the government of the Union is restrained from creating a corporation, as a means for performing its functions, on the single reason that the creation of a corporation is an act of sovereignty; if the sufficiency of this reason be acknowledged, there would be some difficulty in sustaining the authority of Congress to pass other laws for the accomplishment of the same objects.

The government which has a right to do an act, and has imposed on it the duty of performing that act, must, according to the dictates of reason, be allowed to select the means; and those who contend that it may not select any appropriate means, that one particular mode of effecting the object is excepted, take upon themselves the burden of establishing that exception.

The creation of a corporation, it is said, appertains to sovereignty. This is admitted. But to what portion of sovereignty does it appertain? Does it belong to one more than to another? In America, the powers of sovereignty are divided between the government of the Union, and those of the States. They are each sovereign, with respect to the objects committed to it, and neither sovereign with respect to the objects committed to the other. We cannot comprehend that train of reasoning which would maintain, that the extent of power granted by the people is to be ascertained, not by the nature and terms of the grant, but by its date. Some State constitutions were formed *before*, some *since* that of the United States. We cannot believe that their relation to each other is in any degree dependent upon this circumstance. Their respective powers must, we think, be precisely the same as if they had been formed at the same time. Had they been formed at the same time, and had the people conferred on the general government the power contained in the constitution, and on the States the whole residuum of power, would it have been asserted that the government of the Union was not sovereign with respect to those objects which were entrusted to it, in relation to which its laws were declared to be supreme? If this could not have been asserted, we cannot well comprehend the process of reasoning which maintains, that a power appertaining to sovereignty cannot be connected with that vast portion of it which is granted to the general government, so far as it is calculated to subserve the legitimate objects of that government. The power of creating a corporation, though appertaining to sovereignty, is not, like the power of making war, or levying taxes, or of regulating commerce, a great substantive and independent power, which cannot be implied as incidental to other powers, or used as a means of executing them. It is never the end for which other powers are exercised, but a means by which other objects are accomplished. No contributions are made to charity for the sake of an incorporation, but a corporation is created to administer the charity; no seminary of learning is instituted in order to be incorporated, but the corporate character is conferred to subserve the purposes of education. No city was ever built with the sole object of being incorporated, but is incorporated as affording the best means of being well governed. The power of creating a corporation is never used for its own sake, but for the purpose of effecting something else. No sufficient reason is, therefore, perceived, why it may not pass as incidental to those powers which are expressly given, if it be a direct mode of executing them.

But the constitution of the United States has not left the right of Congress to employ the necessary means, for the execution of the powers conferred on the government, to general reasoning. To its enumeration of powers is added that of making "all laws which shall be necessary and proper, for carrying into execution the foregoing powers, and all other powers vested by this constitution, in the government of the United States, or in any department thereof."

The counsel for the State of Maryland have urged various

arguments, to prove that this clause, though in terms a grant of power, is not so in effect; but is really restrictive of the general right, which might otherwise be implied, of selecting means for executing the enumerated powers.

In support of this proposition, they have found it necessary to contend, that this clause was inserted for the purpose of conferring on Congress the power of making laws. That, without it, doubts might be entertained, whether Congress could exercise its powers in the form of legislation.

But could this be the object for which it was inserted? A government is created by the people, having legislative, executive, and judicial powers. Its legislative powers are vested in a Congress, which is to consist of a Senate and House of Representatives. Each house may determine the rule of its proceedings; and it is declared that every bill which shall have passed both houses, shall, before it becomes a law, be presented to the President of the United States. The 7th section describes the course of proceedings, by which a bill shall become a law; and, then, the 8th section enumerates the powers of Congress. Could it be necessary to say, that a legislature should exercise legislative powers, in the shape of legislation? After allowing each house to prescribe its own course of proceeding, after describing the manner in which a bill should become a law, would it have entered into the mind of a single member of the Convention, that an express power to make laws was necessary to enable the legislature to make them? That a legislature, endowed with legislative powers, can legislate, is a proposition too self-evident to have been questioned.

But the argument on which most reliance is placed, is drawn from the peculiar language of this clause. Congress is not empowered by it to make all laws, which may have relation to the powers conferred on the government, but such only as may be *"necessary and proper"* for carrying them into execution. The word *"necessary,"* is considered as controlling the whole sentence, and as limiting the right to pass laws for the execution of the granted powers, to such as are indispensable, and without which the power would be nugatory. That it excludes the choice of means, and leaves to Congress, in each case, that only which is most direct and simple.

Is it true, that this is the sense in which the word "necessary" is always used? Does it always import an absolute physical necessity, so strong, that one thing, to which another may be termed necessary, cannot exist without that other? We think it does not. If reference be had to its use, in the common affairs of the world, or in approved authors, we find that it frequently imports no more than that one thing is convenient, or useful, or essential to another. To employ the means necessary to an end, is generally understood as employing any means calculated to produce the end, and not as being confined to those single means, without which the end would be entirely unattainable. Such is the character of human language, that no word conveys to the mind, in all situations, one single definite idea; and nothing is more common than to use words in a figurative sense. Almost all compositions contain words, which, taken in their rigorous sense, would convey a meaning different from that which is obviously intended. It is essential to just construction, that many words which import something excessive, should be understood in a more mitigated sense—in that sense which common usage justifies. The word "necessary" is of this description. It has not a fixed character peculiar to itself. It admits of all degrees of comparison; and is often connected with other words, which increase or diminish the impression the mind receives of the urgency it imports. A thing may be necessary, very necessary, absolutely or indispensably necessary. To no mind would the same idea be conveyed, by these several phrases. This comment on the word is well illustrated, by the passage cited at the bar, from the 10th section of the 1st article of the constitution. It is, we think, impossible to compare the sentence which prohibits a State from laying "imposts, or duties on imports or exports, except what may be *absolutely* necessary for executing its inspection laws," with that which authorizes Congress "to make all laws which shall be necessary and proper for carrying into execution" the powers of the general government, without feeling a conviction that the convention understood itself to change materially the meaning of the word "necessary," by prefixing the word "absolutely." This word, then, like others, is used in various senses; and, in its construction, the subject, the context, the intention of the person using them, are all to be taken into view.

Let this be done in the case under consideration. The subject is the execution of those great powers on which the welfare of a nation essentially depends. It must have been the intention of those who gave these powers, to insure, as far as human prudence could insure, their beneficial execution. This could not be done by confining the choice of means to such narrow limits as not to leave it in the power of Congress to adopt any which might be appropriate, and which were conducive to the end. This provision is made in a constitution intended to endure for ages to come, and, consequently, to be adapted to the various *crises* of human affairs. To have prescribed the means by which government should, in all future time, execute its powers, would have been to change, entirely, the character of the instrument, and give it the properties of a legal code. It would have been an unwise attempt to provide, by immutable rules, for exigencies which, if foreseen at all, must have been seen dimly, and which can be best provided for as they occur. To have declared that the best means shall not be used, but those alone without which the power given would be nugatory, would have been to deprive the legislature of the capacity to avail itself of experience, to exercise its reason, and to accommodate its legislation to circumstances. If we apply this principle of construction to any of the powers of the government, we shall find it so pernicious in its operation that we shall be compelled to discard it. The powers vested in Congress may certainly be carried into execution, without prescribing an oath of office. The power to exact this security for the faithful performance of duty, is not given, nor is it indispensably necessary. The different departments may be established; taxes may be imposed and collected; armies and navies may be raised and maintained; and money may be borrowed, without requiring an oath of office. It might be argued, with as much plausibility as other incidental powers have been assailed, that the Convention was not unmindful of this subject. The oath which might be exacted—that of fidelity to the constitution—is prescribed, and no other can be required. Yet, he would be charged with insanity who should contend, that the legislature might not superadd, to the oath directed by the constitution, such other oath of office as its wisdom might suggest.

So, with respect to the whole penal code of the United States: whence arises the power to punish in cases not prescribed by the constitution? All admit that the government may, legitimately, punish any violation of its laws; and yet, this is not among the enumerated powers of Congress. The right to enforce the observance of law, by punishing its infraction, might be denied with the more plausibility, because it is expressly given in some cases. Congress is empowered "to provide for the punishment of counterfeiting the securities and current coin of the United States," and "to define and punish piracies and felonies committed on the high seas, and offenses against the law of nations." The several powers of Congress may exist, in a very imperfect state to be sure, but they may exist and be carried into execution, although no punishment should be inflicted in cases where the right to punish is not expressly given.

Take, for example, the power "to establish post offices and post roads." This power is executed by the single act of making the establishment. But, from this has been inferred the power and duty of carrying the mail along the post road, from one post office to another. And, from this implied power, has again been inferred the right to punish those who steal letters from the post office, or rob the mail. It may be said, with some plausibility, that the right to carry the mail, and to punish those who rob it, is not indispensably necessary to the establishment of a post office and post road. This right is indeed essential to the beneficial exercise of the power, but not indispensably necessary to its existence. So, of the punishment of the crimes of stealing or falsifying a record or process of a Court of the United States, or of perjury in such Court. To punish these offenses is certainly conducive to the due administration of justice. But courts may exist, and may decide the causes brought before them, though such crimes escape punishment.

The baneful influence of this narrow construction on all the operations of the government, and the absolute impracticability of maintaining it without rendering the government incompetent to its great objects, might be illustrated by numerous examples drawn from the constitution, and from our laws. The good sense of the public has pronounced, without hesitation, that the power of punishment appertains to sovereignty, and may be exercised whenever the sovereign has a right to act, as incidental to his constitutional powers. It is a means for carrying into execution all sovereign powers, and may be used, although not indispensably necessary. It is a right incidental to the power, and conducive to its beneficial exercise.

If this limited construction of the word "necessary" must be abandoned in order to punish, whence is derived the rule which would reinstate it, when the government would carry its powers into execution by means not vindictive in their nature? If the word "necessary" means "needful," "requisite," "essential," "conducive to," in order to let in the power of punishment for the infraction of law; why is it not equally comprehensive when required to authorize the use of means which facilitate the execution of the powers of government without the infliction of punishment?

In ascertaining the sense in which the word "necessary" is used in this clause of the constitution, we may derive some aid from that with which it is associated. Congress shall have power "to make all laws which shall be necessary and *proper* to carry into execution" the powers of the government. If the word "necessary" was used in that strict and rigorous sense for which the counsel for the State of Maryland contend, it would be an extraordinary departure from the usual course of the human mind, as exhibited in composition, to add a word, the only possible effect of which is to qualify that strict and rigorous meaning; to present to the mind the idea of some choice of means of legislation not straitened and compressed within the narrow limits for which gentlemen contend.

But the argument which most conclusively demonstrates the error of the construction contended for by the counsel for the State of Maryland, is founded on the intention of the Convention, as manifested in the whole clause. To waste time and argument in proving that, without it, Congress might carry its powers into execution, would be not much less idle than to hold a lighted taper to the sun. As little can it be required to prove, that in the absence of this clause, Congress would have some choice of means. That it might employ those which, in its judgment, would most advantageously effect the object to be accomplished. That any means adapted to the end, any means which tended directly to the execution of the constitutional powers of the government, were in themselves constitutional. This clause, as construed by the State of Maryland, would abridge, and almost annihilate this useful and necessary right of the legislature to select its means. That this could not be intended, is, we should think, had it not been already controverted, too apparent for controversy. We think so for the following reasons:

1st. The clause is placed among the powers of Congress, not among the limitations on those powers.

2nd. Its terms purport to enlarge, not to diminish the powers vested in the government. It purports to be an additional power, not a restriction on those already granted. No reason has been, or can be assigned for thus concealing an intention to narrow the discretion of the national legislature under words which purport to enlarge it. The framers of the constitution wished its adoption, and well knew that it would be endangered by its strength, not by its weakness. Had they been capable of using language which would convey to the eye one idea, and, after deep reflection, impress on the mind another, they would rather have disguised the grant of power, than its limitation. If, then, their intention had been, by this clause, to restrain the free use of means which might otherwise have been implied, that intention would have been inserted in another place, and would have been expressed in terms resembling these. "In carrying into execution the foregoing powers, and all others," &c. "no laws shall be passed but such as are necessary and proper." Had the intention been to make this clause restrictive, it would unquestionably have been so in form as well as in effect.

The result of the most careful and attentive consideration bestowed upon this clause is, that if it does not enlarge, it cannot be construed to restrain the powers of Congress, or to impair the right of the legislature to exercise its best judgment in the selection of measures to carry into execution the constitutional powers of the government. If no other motive for its insertion can be suggested, a sufficient one is found in the desire to remove all doubts respecting the right to legislate on that vast mass of incidental powers which must be involved in the constitution, if that instrument be not a splendid bauble.

We admit, as all must admit, that the powers of the government are limited, and that its limits are not to be transcended. But we think the sound construction of the constitution must allow to the national legislature that discretion, with respect to the means by which the powers it confers are to be carried into execution, which will enable that body to perform the high duties assigned to it, in the manner most beneficial to the people. Let the end be legitimate, let it be within the scope of the constitution, and all means which are appropriate, which are plainly adapted to that end, which are not prohibited, but consist with the letter and spirit of the constitution, are constitutional.

That a corporation must be considered as a means not less usual, not of higher dignity, not more requiring a particular specification than other means, has been sufficiently proved. If we look to the origin of corporations, to the manner in which they have been framed in that government from which we have derived most of our legal principles and ideas, or to the uses to which they have been applied, we find no reason to suppose that a constitution, omitting, and wisely omitting, to enumerate all the means for carrying into execution the great powers vested in government, ought to have specified this. Had it been intended to grant this power as one which should be distinct and independent, to be exercised in any case whatever, it would have found a place among the enumerated powers of the government. But being considered merely as a means, to be employed only for the purpose of carrying into execution the given powers, there could be no motive for particularly mentioning it.

The propriety of this remark would seem to be generally acknowledged by the universal acquiescence in the construction which has been uniformly put on the 3rd section of the 4th article of the constitution. The power to "make all needful rules and regulations respecting the territory or other property belonging to the United States," is not more comprehensive, than the power "to make all laws which shall be necessary and proper for carrying into execution" the powers of the government. Yet all admit the constitutionality of a territorial government, which is a corporate body.

If a corporation may be employed indiscriminately with other means to carry into execution the powers of the government, no particular reason can be assigned for excluding the use of a bank, if required for its fiscal operations. To use one, must be within the discretion of Congress, if it be an appropriate mode of executing the powers of government. That it is a convenient, a useful, and essential instrument in the prosecution of its fiscal operations, is not now a subject of controversy. All those who have been concerned in the administration of our finances, have concurred in representing its importance and necessity; and so strongly have they been felt, that statesmen of the first class, whose previous opinions against it had been confirmed by every circumstance which can fix the human judgment, have yielded those opinions to the exigencies of the nation. Under the confederation, Congress, justifying the measure by its necessity, transcended perhaps its powers to obtain the advantage of a bank; and our own legislation attests the universal conviction of the utility of this measure. The time has passed away when it can be necessary to enter into any discussion in order to prove the importance of this instrument, as a means to effect the legitimate objects of the government.

But, were its necessity less apparent, none can deny its being an appropriate measure; and if it is, the degree of its necessity, as has been very justly observed, is to be discussed in another place. Should Congress, in the execution of its powers, adopt measures which are prohibited by the constitution; or should Congress, under the pretext of executing its powers, pass laws for the accomplishment of objects not entrusted to the government; it would become the painful duty of this tribunal, should a case requiring such a decision come before it, to say that such an act was not the law of the land. But where the law is not prohibited, and is really calculated to effect any of the objects entrusted to the government, to undertake here to inquire into the degree of its necessity, would be to pass the line which circumscribes the judicial department, and to tread on legislative ground. This court disclaims all pretensions to such a power.

After this declaration, it can scarcely be necessary to say, that the existence of State banks can have no possible influence on the question. No trace is to be found in the constitution of an intention to create a dependence of the government of the Union on those of the States, for the execution of the great powers assigned to it. Its means are adequate to its ends; and on those means alone was it expected to rely for the accomplishment of its ends. To impose on it the necessity of resorting to means which it cannot control, which another government may furnish or withhold, would render its course precarious, the result of its measures uncertain, and create a dependence on other governments, which might disappoint its most important designs, and is incompatible with the language of the constitution. But were it otherwise, the choice of means implies a right to choose a national bank in preference to State banks, and Congress alone can make the election.

After the most deliberate consideration, it is the unanimous and decided opinion of this Court, that the act to incorporate the Bank of the United States is a law made in pursuance of the constitution, and is a part of the supreme law of the land.

The branches, proceeding from the same stock, and being conducive to the complete accomplishment of the object, are equally constitutional. It would have been unwise to locate them in the charter, and it would be unnecessarily inconvenient to employ the legislative power in making those subordinate arrangements. The great duties of the bank are prescribed; those duties require branches; and the bank itself may, we think, be safely trusted with the selection of places where those branches shall be fixed; reserving always to the government the right to require that a branch shall be located where it may be deemed necessary.

It being the opinion of the Court, that the act incorporating the bank is constitutional; and that the power of establishing a branch in the State of Maryland might be properly exercised by the bank itself, we proceed to inquire—

2. Whether the State of Maryland may, without violating the constitution, tax that branch?

That the power of taxation is one of vital importance; that it is retained by the States; that it is not abridged by the grant of a similar power to the government of the Union; that it is to be concurrently exercised by the two governments: are truths which have never been denied. But, such is the paramount character of the constitution, that its capacity to withdraw any subject from the action of even this power, is admitted. The States are expressly forbidden to lay any duties on imports or exports, except what may be absolutely necessary for executing their inspection laws. If the obligation of this prohibition must be conceded—if it may restrain a State from the exercise of its taxing power on imports and exports; the same paramount character would seem to restrain, as it certainly may restrain, a State from such other exercise of this power, as is in its nature incompatible with, and repugnant to, the constitutional laws of the Union. A law, absolutely repugnant to another, as entirely repeals that other as if express terms of repeal were used.

On this ground the counsel for the bank place its claim to be exempted from the power of a State to tax its operations. There is no express provision for the case, but the claim has been sustained on a principle which so entirely pervades the constitution, is so intermixed with the materials which compose it, so interwoven with its web, so blended with its texture, as to be incapable of being separated from it, without rending it into shreds.

This great principle is, that the constitution and the laws made in pursuance thereof are supreme; that they control the constitution and laws of the respective States, and cannot be controlled by them. From this, which may be almost termed an axiom, other propositions are deduced as corollaries, on the truth or error of which, and on their application to this case, the cause has been supposed to depend. These are, 1st. that a power to create implies a power to preserve. 2nd. That a power to destroy, if wielded by a different hand, is hostile to, and incompatible with these powers to create and to preserve. 3d. That where this repugnancy exists, that authority which is supreme must control, not yield to that over which it is supreme.

These propositions, as abstract truths, would, perhaps, never be controverted. Their application to this case, however, has been denied; and, both in maintaining the affirmative and the negative, a splendor of eloquence, and strength of argument, seldom, if ever, surpassed, have been displayed.

The power of Congress to create, and of course to continue, the bank, was the subject of the preceding part of this opinion; and is no longer to be considered as questionable.

That the power of taxing it by the States may be exercised so as to destroy it, is too obvious to be denied. But taxation is said to be an absolute power, which acknowledges no other limits than those expressly prescribed in the constitution, and like sovereign power of every other description, is trusted to the discretion of those who use it. But the very terms of this argument admit that the sovereignty of the State, in the article of taxation itself, is subordinate to, and may be controlled by the constitution of the United States. How far it has been controlled by that instrument must be a question of construction. In making this construction, no principle not declared, can be admissable, which would defeat the legitimate operations of a supreme government. It is of the very essence of supremacy to remove all obstacles to its action within its own sphere, and so to modify every power vested in subordinate governments, as to exempt its own operations from their own influence. This effect need not be stated in terms. It is so involved in the declaration of supremacy, so necessarily implied in it, that the expression of it could not make it more certain. We must, therefore, keep it in view while construing the constitution.

The argument on the part of the State of Maryland, is, not that the States may directly resist a law of Congress, but that they may exercise their acknowledged powers upon it, and that the constitution leaves them this right in the confidence that they will not abuse it.

Before we proceed to examine this argument, and to subject it to the test of the constitution, we must be permitted to bestow a few considerations on the nature and extent of this original right of taxation, which is acknowledged to remain with the States. It is admitted that the power of taxing the people and their property is essential to the very existence of government, and may be legitimately exercised on the objects to which it is applicable, to the utmost extent to which the government may chuse to carry it. The only security against the abuse of this power, is found in the structure of the government itself. In imposing a tax the legislature acts upon its constituents. This is in general a sufficient security against erroneous and oppressive taxation.

The people of a State, therefore, give to their government a right of taxing themselves and their property, and as the exigencies of government cannot be limited, they prescribe no limits to the exercise of this right, resting confidently on the interest of the legislator, and on the influence of the constituents over their representative, to guard them against its abuse. But the means employed by the government of the Union have no such security, nor is the right of a State to tax them sustained by the same theory. Those means are not given by the people of a particular State, not given by the constituents of the legislature, which claim the right to tax them, but by the people of all the States. They are given by all, for the benefit of all—and upon theory, should be subjected to that government only which belongs to all.

It may be objected to this definition, that the power of taxation is not confined to the people and property of a State. It may be exercised upon every object brought within its jurisdiction.

This is true. But to what source do we trace this right? It is obvious, that it is an incident of sovereignty, and is co-extensive with that to which it is an incident. All subjects over which the sovereign power of a State extends, are objects of taxation; but those over which it does not extend, are, upon the soundest principles, exempt from taxation. This proposition may almost be pronounced self-evident.

The sovereignty of a State extends to every thing which exists by its own authority, or is introduced by its permission; but does it extend to those means which are employed by Congress to carry into execution powers conferred on that body by the people of the United States? We think it demonstrable that it does not. Those powers are not given by the people of a single State. They are given by the people of the United States, to a government whose laws, made in pursuance of the constitution, are declared to be supreme. Consequently, the people of a single State cannot confer a sovereignty which will extend over them.

If we measure the power of taxation residing in a State, by the extent of sovereignty which the people of a single State possess, and can confer on its government, we have an intelligible standard, applicable to every case to which the power may be applied. We have a principle which leaves the power of taxing the people and property of a State unimpaired; which leaves to a State the command of all its resources, and which places beyond its reach, all those powers which are conferred by the people of the United States on the government of the Union, and all those means which are given for the purpose of carrying those powers into execution. We have a principle which is safe for the States, and safe for the Union. We are relieved, as we ought to be, from clashing sovereignty; from interfering powers; from a repugnancy between a right in one government to pull down what there is an acknowledged right in another to build up; from the incompatibility of a right in one government to destroy what there is a right in another to preserve. We are not driven to the perplexing inquiry, so unfit for the judicial department, what degree of taxation is the legitimate use, and what degree may amount to the abuse of the power. The attempt to use it on the means employed by the government of the Union, in pursuance of the constitution, is itself an abuse, because it is the usurpation of a power which the people of a single State cannot give.

We find, then, on just theory, a total failure of this original right to tax the means employed by the government of the Union, for the execution of its powers. The right never existed, and the question whether it has been surrendered, cannot arise.

But, waiving this theory for the present, let us resume the inquiry, whether this power can be exercised by the respective States, consistently with a fair construction of the constitution?

That the power to tax involves the power to destroy; that the power to destroy may defeat and render useless the power to create; that there is a plain repugnance, in conferring on one government a power to control the constitutional measures of another, which other, with respect to those very measures, is declared to be supreme over that which exerts the control, are propositions not to be denied. But all inconsistencies are to be reconciled by the magic of the word CONFIDENCE. Taxation, it is said, does not necessarily and unavoidably destroy. To carry it to the excess of destruction would be an abuse, to presume which, would banish that confidence which is essential to all government.

But is this a case of confidence? Would the people of any one State trust those of another with a power to control the most insignificant operations of their State government? We know they would not. Why, then, should we suppose that the people of any one State should be willing to trust those of another with a power to control the operations of a government to which they have confided their most important and most valuable interests? In the legislature of the Union alone, are all represented. The legislature of the Union alone, therefore, can be trusted by the people with the power of controlling measures which concern all, in the confidence that it will not be abused. This, then, is not a case of confidence, and we must consider it as it really is.

If we apply the principle for which the State of Maryland contends, to the constitution generally, we shall find it capable of changing totally the character of that instrument. We shall find it capable of arresting all the measures of the government, and of prostrating it at the foot of the States. The American people have declared their constitution, and the laws made in pursuance thereof, to be supreme; but this principle would transfer the supremacy, in fact, to the States.

If the States may tax one instrument, employed by the government in the execution of its powers, they may tax any and every other instrument. They may tax the mail; they may tax the mint; they may tax patent rights; they may tax the papers of the custom-house; they may tax judicial process; they may tax all the means employed by the government, to an excess which would defeat all the ends of government. This was not intended by the American people. They did not design to make their government dependent on the States.

Gentlemen say, they do not claim the right to extend State taxation to these objects. They limit their pretensions to property. But on what principle is this distinction made? Those who make it have furnished no reason for it, and the principle for which they contend denies it. They contend that the power of taxation has no other limit than is found in the 10th section of the 1st article of the constitution; that, with respect to every thing else, the power of the States is supreme, and admits of no control. If this be true, the distinction between property and other subjects to which the power of taxation is applicable, is merely arbitrary, and can never be sustained. This is not all. If the controling power of the States be established; if their supremacy as to taxation be acknowledged; what is to restrain their exercising this control in any shape they may please to give it? Their sovereignty is not confined to taxation. That is not the only mode in which it might be displayed. The question is, in truth, a question of supremacy; and if the right of the States to tax the means employed by the general government be conceded, the declaration that the constitution, and the laws made in pursuance thereof, shall be the supreme law of the land, is empty and unmeaning declamation.

In the course of the argument, the *Federalist* has been quoted; and the opinions expressed by the authors of that work have been justly supposed to be entitled to great respect in expounding the constitution. No tribute can be paid to them which exceeds their merit; but in applying their opinions to the cases which may arise in the progress of our government, a right to judge of their correctness must be retained; and, to understand the argument, we must examine the proposition it maintains, and the objections against which it is directed. The subject of those numbers, from which passages have been cited, is the unlimited power of taxation which is vested in the general government. The objection to this unlimited power, which the argument seeks to remove, is stated with fullness and clearness. It is, "that an indefinite power of taxation in the latter (the government of the Union) might, and probably would, in time, deprive the former (the government of the States) of the means of providing for their own necessities; and would subject them entirely to the mercy of the national legislature. As the laws of the Union are to become the supreme law of the land; as it is to have power to pass all laws that may be necessary for carrying into execution the authorities with which it is proposed to vest it; the national government might at any time abolish the taxes imposed for State objects, upon the pretence of an interference with its own. It might allege a necessity for doing this, in order to give efficacy to the national revenues; and thus all the resources of taxation might, by degrees, become the subjects of federal monopoly, to the entire exclusion and destruction of the State governments."

The objections to the constitution which are noticed in these numbers, were to the undefined power of the government to tax, not to the incidental privilege of exempting its own measures from State taxation. The consequences apprehended from this undefined power were, that it would absorb all the objects of taxation, "to the exclusion and destruction of the State governments." The arguments of the *Federalist* are intended to prove the fallacy of these apprehensions; not to prove that the government was incapable of executing any of its powers, without exposing the means it employed to the embarrassments of State taxation. Arguments urged against these objections, and these apprehensions, are to be understood as relating to the points they mean to prove. Had the authors of those excellent essays been asked, whether they contended for that construction of the constitution, which would place within the reach of the States those measures which the government might adopt for the execution of its powers; no man, who has read their instructive pages, will hesitate to admit, that their answer must have been in the negative.

It has also been insisted, that, as the power of taxation in the general and State governments is acknowledged to be concurrent, every argument which would sustain the right of the general government to tax banks chartered by the States, will equally sustain the right of the States to tax banks chartered by the general government.

But the two cases are not on the same reason. The people of all the States have created the general government, and have conferred upon it the general power of taxation. The people of all the States, and the States themselves, are represented in Congress, and, by their representatives, exercise this power. When they tax the chartered institutions of the States, they tax their constituents; and these taxes must be uniform. But, when a State taxes the operations of the government of the United States, it acts upon institutions created, not by their own constituents, but by people over whom they claim no control. It acts upon the measures of a government created by others as well as themselves, for the benefit of others in common with themselves. The difference is that which always exists, and always must exist, between the action of the whole on a part, and the action of a part on the whole—between the laws of a government declared to be supreme, and those of a government which, when in opposition to those laws, is not supreme.

But if the full application of this argument could be admitted, it might bring into question the right of Congress to tax the State banks, and could not prove the right of the States to tax the Bank of the United States.

The Court has bestowed on this subject its most deliberate consideration. The result is a conviction that the States have no power, by taxation or otherwise, to retard, impede, burden, or in any manner control, the operations of the constitutional laws enacted by Congress to carry into execution the powers vested in the general government. This is, we think, the unavoidable consequence of that supremacy which the constitution has declared.

We are unanimously of opinion, that the law passed by the legislature of Maryland, imposing a tax on the Bank of the United States, is unconstitutional and void.

This opinion does not deprive the States of any resources which they originally possessed. It does not extend to a tax paid by the real property of the bank, in common with the other real property within the State, nor to a tax imposed on the interest which the citizens of Maryland may hold in this institution, in common with other property of the same description throughout the State. But this is a tax on the operations of the bank, and is, consequently, a tax on the operation of an instrument employed by the government of the Union to carry its powers into execution. Such a tax must be unconstitutional.

JUDGMENT. This cause came on to be heard on the transcript of the record of the Court of Appeals of the State of Maryland, and was argued by counsel. On consideration whereof, it is the opinion of this Court, that the Act of the Legislature of Maryland is contrary to the Constitution of the United States, and void; and, therefore, that the said Court of Appeals of the State of Maryland erred in affirming the judgment of the Baltimore County Court, in which judgment was rendered against James W. M'Culloch; but that the said Court of Appeals of Maryland ought to have reversed the said judgment of the said Baltimore County Court, and ought to have given judgment for the said appellant, M'Culloch. It is, therefore, Adjudged and Ordered, that the said judgment of the said Court of Appeals of the State of Maryland in this case, be, and the same hereby is, reversed and annulled. And this Court, proceeding to render such judgment as the said Court of Appeals should have rendered; it is further Adjudged and Ordered, that the judgment of the said Baltimore County Court be reversed and annulled, and that judgment be entered in the said Baltimore County Court for the said James W. M'Culloch.

A Virginian's "Amphictyon" Essays

Richmond Enquirer, March 30–April 2, 1819

The editor of the Richmond Enquirer, *Thomas Ritchie, made a special effort to alert his readers to the importance of the "Amphictyon" and "Hampden" essays. At the beginning of each series, he made editorial comments of considerable political as well as journalistic weight: Ritchie was, with his cousin Spencer Roane, a leader of the Richmond Junto.*

Ritchie's introduction to "Amphictyon" reads: "We cannot too earnestly press upon our readers, the following exposition of the alarming errors of the Supreme Court of the United States in their late interpretation of the Constitution. We conceive those errors to be most alarming, and this exposition most satisfactory. Whenever state rights are threatened or invaded, Virginia will not be the last to sound the tocsin. Again, we earnestly recommend the following to the attention of the reader." Ritchie's opening remarks to the "Hampden" essays are on p. 106. The Ritchie paragraphs were not lost on Marshall: the Chief Justice commented on them in both the Philadelphia Union *and the* Alexandria Gazette *essays.—GG.*

I

To the Editor of the Enquirer:

SIR—I have read with considerable attention the opinion pronounced by the Chief Justice of the U.S. in the case of McCulloh against the state of Maryland. In that opinion we are informed, 1st. That it is the *unanimous* and decided opinion of the Supreme

Court, that the act to incorporate the Bank of the U.S. is a law made in pursuance of the Constitution, and is a part of the supreme law of the land; and, 2dly. That the Court is also unanimously of opinion that the law of Maryland imposing a tax on the Bank of Maryland, is unconstitutional and void. We are not informed whether the whole court united in the course of reasoning adopted by the Chief Justice, nor whether they all accorded in the various positions and principles which he advanced. It may be, that some of them admitted that the bank law is constitutional, and yet did not think proper to deny that the several states are parties to the federal compact: it may be, that some of them, without giving to the term "necessary" the liberal and latitudinous construction, attached to it by the Chief Justice, and before him by Mr. Secretary Hamilton, may yet have thought that the measure of incorporating a bank was "necessary and proper" for carrying into execution some of the specific powers granted to Congress; or some of them may have believed that it was for Congress to have judged of that "necessity, and propriety," and having exercised their undoubted functions in so deciding, that it was not consistent with judicial modesty to say "there was no such necessity," and thus to arrogate to themselves a right of putting their *veto* upon a law; or it may be, that some members of the court thought the bank law "necessary and proper" to carry into effect one power, whilst others thought that it was the instrument for effectuating another and a different power. Although they have all arrived at the same place, they may have travelled thither by different roads; although they have come to the same conclusion, yet their reasons may have been considerably variant from each other. I confess, that as a citizen, I should have been better pleased to have seen the separate opinions of the judges. The occasion called for *seriatim* opinions. On this great constitutional question, affecting very much the rights of the several states composing our confederacy, the decision of which abrogated the law of one state, and is supposed to have formed a rule for the future conduct of other states, the people had surely a right to expect that each judge should assign his own reasons for the vote which he gave. The court seems to have thought that it was sitting as an umpire to decide between the conflicting claims of a sovereign state on the one hand, and the whole United States on the other, and yet the judges decline the expression of the principles on which they have separately formed their judgments! Having thus declined the declaration of their separate opinions, we are driven, however reluctantly, to the conclusion that each judge approves of each argument and position advanced by the chief justice.

That this opinion is very able, every one must admit. This was to have been expected, proceeding as it does from a man of the most profound legal attainments, and upon a subject which has employed his thoughts, his tongue, and his pen, as a politician, and an historian, for more than thirty years. The subject too, is one which has, perhaps more than any other, heretofore drawn a broad line of distinction between the two great parties in this country, in which line no one has taken a more distinguished and decided rank than the judge who has thus expounded the supreme law of the land.—It is not in my power to carry on a contest upon such a subject with a man of his gigantic powers, but I trust that it will not be thought rash or presumptuous to endeavor to point out the consequences of some of the doctrines maintained by the supreme court, and to oppose to their adjudication some of the principles which have heretofore been advocated by the republican party in this country.

There are two principles advocated and decided on by the supreme court, which appear to me to endanger the very existence of state rights. The first is the denial that the powers of the federal government were delegated by the states; and the second is, that the grant of powers to that government, and particularly the grant of powers "necessary and proper" to carry the other powers into effect, ought to be construed in a liberal, rather than a restricted sense. Both of these principles tend directly to consolidation of the states, and to strip them of some of the most important attributes of their sovereignty. If the Congress of the United States should think proper to legislate to the full extent, upon the principles now adjudicated by the supreme court, it is difficult to say how small would be the remnant of power left in the hands of the state authorities.

The first position, that the powers of the federal government are not delegated by the states, or in other words that the states are not parties to the compact, is untenable in itself, and fatal in its consequences. But for what purpose, I will ask, did the federal court decide that question? To ascertain whether the bank law was consistent with the constitution, or not, it was not necessary, I apprehend, that the court should have enquired into the source from whence the authority of the government was derived. Whether the powers of the federal government were delegated to it, by the states in their sovereign capacity, or by the people, can make but little difference as to the extent of those powers. In either case, it is still true that the powers of that government are limited by the charter which called it into existence; in either case, it is true that the departments of that government cannot either separately or conjointly transcend those limits without affecting the rights and liberties of the states, or of the people: in either case, the construction of the words of the constitution ought to be the same. The decision of that question then was unnecessary; the court travelled out of the record to decide a point not necessarily growing out of it; the decision of that point is therefore merely *obiter*, extra-judicial, and not more binding or obligatory than the opinion of any other six intelligent members of the community. The opinion is erroneous. The several states did delegate to the federal government its powers, and they are parties to the compact. Who gave birth to the constitution? The history of the times, and the instrument itself furnish the ready answer to the question. The federal convention of 1787 was composed of delegates appointed by the respective state legislatures; and who voted by states; the constitution was submitted on their recommendation, to conventions elected by the people of the several states, that is to say, to the states themselves in their highest political, and sovereign authority: by those separate conventions, representing, not the whole mass of the population of the United States, but the people only within the limits of the respective sovereign states, the constitution was adopted and brought into existence. The individuality of the several states was still kept up when they assembled in convention: their sovereignty was still preserved, and the only effect of the adoption of the constitution was to take from one set of their agents and servants, to wit, the state governments, a certain portion of specified powers, and to delegate that same portion to another set of servants and agents, then newly created, namely, the federal government. If the powers of the federal government are to be viewed as the grant of the people, without regard to the distinctive features of the states, then it would follow that if a majority of the whole sovereign population of the United States had ratified the constitution, it would immediately have been binding on the minority, although that minority should consist of every individual in one or more states. But we know that such was not the case. Each state was an independent political society. The constitution was not binding on any state, even the smallest, without its own free and voluntary consent. Although nineteen-twentieths of the whole people of the U. States, had approved of, and adopted the constitution, yet it was not a constitution obligatory on Rhode Island, until that small state became a party to it by its own act. The respective states then in their sovereign capacity did delegate to the federal government its powers, and in so doing were parties to the compact.—The states not only gave birth to the constitution, but its life depends upon the existence of the state governments.—The Senate derives its being from them. The President is elected by persons who are as to numbers partly chosen on the federal principle. Destroy the state governments, and you by the same blow destroy the Senate, and with it the constitution. Again, how may this constitution be amended and reformed? By the legislatures of three-fourths of the states, or by conventions of the same number of states in the manner provided by the 5th article.—The states then gave birth to the constitution; they support its existence, and they alone are capable of reforming or of changing its form and substance, and yet we are informed by a solemn adjudication that its powers are not derived from that source, and consequently that they are not parties to it!—This doctrine now solemnly promulgated by the highest judicial tribunal of that government, is not however a novelty in our history. In the years 1798 and '99, after the Congress of that time had by the force of implication passed a sedition law, and vested the President with arbitrary and despotic powers over the persons of alien friends, after many political writers, and some of the federal courts had advocated the absurd and dangerous doctrine that the common law of England made a part of the law of these states, in their united and national capacity, then it was that this doctrine, which denies that the states are parties to the federal compact, was pressed with great zeal and ability. Having attempted to place shackles on the press, the glorious work could not be completed without imposing moral fetters on the independent minds of the several state legislatures. The doctrine, however, was exposed and refuted, and I did not expect that it would be brought forward at this day under the supposed sanction of the highest judicial authority.

The doctrine, if admitted to be true, would be of fatal consequence to the rights and freedom of the people of the states. If the states are not parties to the compact, the legislatures of the several states, who annually bring together the feelings, the wishes, and the opinions of the people within their respective limits, would not have a right to canvass the public measures of the Congress, or of the President, nor to remonstrate against the encroachments of power, nor to resist the advances of usurpation, tyranny and oppression. They would no longer be hailed as the sentinels of the public liberty, nor as the protectors of their own rights. Every government, which has ever yet been established, feels a disposition to increase its own powers. Without the restraints which are imposed by an enlightened public opinion, this tendency will inevitably conduct the freest government to the exercise of tyrannic power. If the right of resistance be denied, or taken away, despotism inevitably follows. It has however been supposed by some, that the constitution has provided a remedy for every evil: that the right of the state governments to protest against, or to resist encroachments on their authority is taken away, and transferred to the federal judiciary, whose power extends to all cases arising under the constitution; that the supreme court is the umpire to decide between the states on the one side, and the United States on the other, in all questions touching the constitutionality of laws, or acts of the Executive. There are many cases which can never be brought before that tribunal, and I do humbly conceive that the states never could have committed an act of such egregious folly as to agree that their umpire should be altogether appointed and paid by the other party. The supreme court may be a perfectly impartial tribunal to decide between two states, but cannot be considered in that point of view when the contest lies between the United States, and one of its members.

That I am not singular in the opinion which I entertain upon this subject, is very certain. There have been two judicial decisions in two of the largest states of the union, which expressly decide that the several states are parties to the federal compact. I refer to the decision of the supreme court of Pennsylvania in the case of the commonwealth against William Cobbett, reported in the 3d volume of Dallas; and to the decision of the Court of appeals of

Virginia in Hunter against Martin, reported in 4th Munford.*—
But I cannot forbear on this occasion from bringing to my aid
a part of the report of a committee of the House of Delegates of
Virginia in the year 1799, in which this subject is enforced with
reasoning the most cogent and explained in language the most
perspicuous. It will be recollected that in the session of the legislature of 1798, sundry resolutions had been adopted complaining
of sundry acts of usurpation on the part of congress, and particularly of the alien and sedition laws. Those resolutions having been
disapproved of, by most of the other state legislatures, became
the subject of examination at the succeeding session, and produced
that remarkable commentary which has generally been known by
the name of Madison's report. The third resolution is as follows:

That this assembly doth explicitly and peremptorily declare that it
views the powers of the federal government, as resulting from the compact, to which the states are parties, as limited by the plain sense and
intention of the instrument constituting that compact; as no farther
valid than they are authorized by the grants enumerated in that compact; and that in case of a deliberate, palpable and dangerous exercise
of other powers, not granted by the said compact, the states who are
parties thereto, have the right, and they are in duty bound, to interpose,
for arresting the progress of the evil, and for maintaining within their
respective limits, the authorities, rights and liberties appertaining to
them.

---

* That the state governments are parties to the federal compact, and able
to combine for the purpose of protecting their common liberty, seems to have
been admitted by the author of the letters of Publius. "It may safely be received as an axiom in our political system, that the state governments will in
all possible contingencies, afford complete security against invasions of the
public liberty by the national authority. Projects of usurpation cannot be
masked under pretences, so likely to escape the penetration of select bodies
of men, as of the people at large. The legislatures will have better means of
information—*they can discover danger at a distance*; and possessing all the
organs of civil power and the confidence of the people, they can at once adopt
a regular plan of opposition, in which they can combine all the resources of
the community. They can readily communicate with each other in the different states; and unite their common forces, for the protection of their common liberty." (See Federalist, No. 28.)

On this resolution, the committee have bestowed all the attention which its importance merits: they have scanned it not merely with a strict, but with a severe eye; and they feel confidence in pronouncing, that in its just and fair construction, it is unexceptionably true in its several positions, as well as constitutional and conclusive in its inferences.

The resolution declares, *first*, that "it views the powers of the Federal Government, as resulting from the compact to which the states are parties," in other words, that the federal powers are derived from the constitution, and that the constitution is a compact to which the states are parties.

Clear as the position must seem, that the federal powers are derived from the Constitution, and from that alone, the committee are not unapprized of a late doctrine which opens another source of federal powers, not less extensive and important, than it is new and unexpected. The examination of this doctrine will be most conveniently connected with a review of a succeeding resolution. The committee satisfy themselves here with briefly remarking, that in all the contemporary discussions and comments, which the Constitution underwent, it was constantly justified and recommended on the ground, that the powers not given to the government, were withheld from it; & that if any doubt could have existed on this subject, under the original text of the Constitution, it is removed as far as words could remove it, by the 12th [10th] amendment, now a part of the Constitution, which expressly declares, "that the powers not delegated to the United States, by the Constitution, nor prohibited by it to the states, are reserved to the states respectively, or to the people."

The other position involved in this branch of the resolution, namely, "that the states are parties to the Constitution or compact," is in the judgment of the committee, equally free from objection. It is indeed true that the term "States," is sometimes used in a vague sense, and sometimes in different senses, according to the subject to which it is applied. Thus it sometimes means the separate sections of territory occupied by the political societies within each; sometimes the particular governments, established by those societies; sometimes those societies as organized into those particular governments; and lastly, it means the people composing those political societies, in their highest sovereign capacity. Although it might be wished that the perfection of language admitted less diversity in the signification of the same words, yet little inconveniency is produced by it, where the true sense can be collected with certainty from the different applications. In the present instance whatever different constructions of the term "States," in the resolution may have been entertained, all will at least concur in that last mentioned; because in that sense, the Constitution was submitted to the "States." In that sense the "States" ratified it; and in that sense of the term "States," they are consequently parties to the compact from which the powers of the Federal Government result.

The next position is, that the General Assembly views the powers of the Federal Government, "as limited by the plain sense and intention of the instrument constituting that compact," and "as no farther valid than they are authorized by the grants therein enumerated." It does not seem possible than any just objection can lie against either of these clauses. The first amounts merely to a declaration that the compact ought to have the interpretation plainly intended by the parties to it; the other, to a declaration, that it ought to have the execution and effect intended by them. If the powers granted, be valid, it is solely because they are granted; and if the granted powers are valid, because granted, all other powers not granted, must not be valid.

The resolution having taken this view of the federal compact, proceeds to infer, "that in case of a deliberate, palpable, and dangerous exercise of other powers not granted by the said compact, the states who are parties thereto, have the right, and are in duty bound to interpose for arresting the progress of the evil, and for maintaining within their respective limits, the authorities, rights and liberties appertaining to them."

It appears to your committee to be a plain principle, founded in common sense, illustrated by common practice, and essential to the nature of compacts; that where resort can be had to no tribunal superior to the authority of the parties, the parties themselves must be the rightful judges in the last resort, whether the bargain made, has been pursued or violated. The Constitution of the United States was formed by the sanction of the states, given by each in its sovereign capacity. It adds to the stability and dignity, as well as to the authority of the Constitution, that it rests on this legitimate and solid foundation. The states then being the parties to the constitutional compact, and in their sovereign capacity, it follows of necessity, that there can be no tribunal above their authority, to decide in the last resort, whether the compact made by them violated; and consequently that as the parties to it, they must themselves decide in the last resort, such questions as may be of sufficient magnitude to require their interposition.

It does not follow, however, that because the States as sovereign parties to their constitutional compact, must ultimately decide whether it has been violated, that such a decision ought to be interposed either in a hasty manner, or on doubtful and inferior occasions. Even in the case of ordinary conventions between different nations, where, by the strict rule of interpretation, a breach of a part may be deemed a breach of the whole; every part being deemed a condition of every other part, and of the whole, it is always laid down that the breach must be both wilful and material to justify an application of the rule. But in the case of an intimate and constitutional union, like that of the United States, it is evident that the interposition of the parties, in their sovereign capacity, can be called for by occasions only, deeply and essentially affecting the vital principles of their political system.

The resolution has accordingly guarded against any misapprehension of its object, by expressly requiring for such an interposition "the case of a *deliberate, palpable,* and *dangerous* breach of the Constitution, by the exercise of *powers not granted* by it." It must be a case, not of a light and transient nature, but of a nature *dangerous* to the great purposes for which the Constitution was established. It must be a case moreover not obscure or doubtful in its construction, but plain and *palpable*. Lastly, it must be a case not resulting from a partial consideration, or hasty determination; but a case stampt with a final consideration and *deliberate* adherence. It is not necessary, because the resolution does not require, that the question should be discussed, how far the exercise of any particular power, ungranted by the Constitution, would justify the interposition of the parties to it. As cases might easily be stated, which none would contend, ought to fall within that description: cases on the other hand, might, with equal ease, be stated, so flagrant and so fatal as to unite every opinion in placing them within the description.

But the resolution has done more than guard against misconstruction, by expressly referring to cases of a *deliberate, palpable,* and *dangerous* nature. It specifies the object of the interposition which it contemplates, to be solely that of arresting the progress of the *evil of* usurpation, and of maintaining the authorities, rights and liberties appertaining to the states, as parties to the Constitution.

From this view of the resolution, it would seem inconceivable that it can incur any just disapprobation from those, who laying aside all momentary impressions, and recollecting the genuine source and object of the Federal Constitution, shall candidly and accurately interpret the meaning of the General Assembly. If the deliberate exercise of dangerous powers, palpably withheld by the Constitution, could not justify the parties to it, in interposing even so far as to arrest the progress of the evil, and thereby to preserve the Constitution itself, as well as to provide for the safety of the parties to it; there would be an end to all relief from usurped power, and a direct subversion of the rights specified or recognized under all the State Constitutions, as well as a plain denial of the fundamental principle on which our independence itself was declared.

But it is objected that the judicial authority is to be regarded as the sole expositor of the Constitution, in the last resort; and it may be asked for what reason, the declaration by the General Assembly, supposing it to be theoretically true, could be required at the present day and in so solemn a manner.

On this objection it might be observed *first*: that there may be instances of usurped power, which the forms of the Constitution would never draw within the controul of the judicial department: secondly, that if the decision of the judiciary be raised above the authority of the sovereign parties to the Constitution, the decisions of the other departments, not carried by the forms of the Constitution before the judiciary, must be equally authoritative and final with the decisions of that department. But the proper answer to the objection is, that the resolution of the General Assembly relates to those great and extraordinary cases, in which all the forms of the Constitution may prove ineffectual against infractions dangerous to the essential rights of the parties to it. The resolution supposes that dangerous powers not delegated, may not only be usurped and executed by the other departments, but that the judicial department also may exercise or sanction dangerous powers beyond the grant of the Constitution; and consequently that the ultimate right of the parties to the Constitution, to judge whether the compact has been dangerously violated, must extend to violations by one delegated authority, as well as by another; by the judiciary, as well as by the executive, or the legislature.

However true therefore it may be that the judicial department, is, in all questions submitted to by the forms of the Constitution, to decide in the last resort. This resort must necessarily be deemed the last in relation to the authorities of other departments of the government; not in relation to the rights of the parties to the Constitutional compact, from which the judicial as well as the other departments hold their delegated trusts. On any other hypothesis, the delegation of judicial power, would annul the authority delegating it; & the concurrence of this department with the others in usurped powers, might subvert forever, and beyond the possible reach of any rightful remedy, the very Constitution, which all were instituted to preserve.

March 30, 1819   AMPHICTYON

II

To the Editor of the Enquirer:

SIR—The other principle contained in the decision of the supreme court, which I apprehend to be of dangerous consequence, and on which I propose to make some remarks, is, that the grant of powers to Congress which may be *"necessary and proper"* to carry into execution the other powers granted to them, or to any department of the government, ought to be construed in a liberal, rather than a restricted sense.

The danger arising from the implied powers has always been seen and felt by the people of the states. Those who opposed the constitution always apprehended, that the powers of the federal government would be enlarged so much by the force of implication as to sweep off every vestige of power from the state governments. The progress of the government from the commencement of it to this day, proves that their fears are not without foundation. To counteract that irresistible tendency in the federal government to enlarge their own dominion, the vigilance of the people and state governments should constantly be exerted.

The 1st clause of the 8th sect. of the constitution is, that "Congress shall have power to lay and collect taxes, duties, imposts, and excises, to pay the debts and provide for the common defence, and *general welfare* of the U. States;" and the last clause of the same section is, "to make all laws which shall be *necessary* and *proper* for carrying into execution the foregoing powers, and all other powers vested by this constitution in the government of the United States, or any department or officer thereof."

Although every one admits that the government of the United States is one of limited powers: that it cannot exercise any, but such as are actually granted, yet so wide is the latitude given to the words "*general welfare*," in one of these clauses, and to the word "*necessary*" in the other, that it will, (if the construction be persisted in) really become a government of almost unlimited powers. If such a consequence will necessarily result from the liberal construction which has been contended for, ought we not to recur to first principles, and change that construction? Although the supreme court has attempted to establish the liberal meaning of the word *necessary* as the settled construction of the constitution, or rather to jostle it from its place, and substitute another word for it, yet I trust that neither the Congress, nor the President, will consider themselves bound by that decision in any *future* case, but will pursue the true meaning of the constitution, and not usurp powers never granted to them.

Why did the framers of the constitution use the word "*necessary*"? They had other words at their command which they might have used, if those other words had conveyed the ideas which they had in their minds. Would they not have said, if they so intended it, that Congress shall have power to make all laws which may be *useful*, or *convenient*, or *conducive to* the effectual execution of the foregoing powers? Will any man assert that the word "*necessary*" is synonymous with those other words? It certainly is not. Why then should we change its meaning?

But, says the chief justice, this word "*necessary*" is susceptible of degrees of comparison, and as a proof that in this clause it is not used to denote the greatest degree of necessity, he instances a part of the 10th section. No state shall lay any duties except what be "*absolutely necessary*" for executing its inspection laws. I apprehend that nothing is gained by this example. What is *absolutely* necessary, is only *positively* necessary, that is, necessary.

It is said that in ascertaining the meaning of the word, "we may derive some aid from that with which it is associated." The word *"proper"* is associated with it, and my inference from that association is directly the reverse of that of the supreme court. The word "proper" has the larger meaning, and the word "necessary" restricts that meaning. Suppose the word "necessary" had been omitted. Then Congress might have made all laws which might be *"proper,"* that is *suitable,* or *fit,* for carrying into execution the other powers; in that case they would have had a wider field of discretion: they would then have only been obliged to enquire what were the suitable means to attain the desired end. But then comes the more important restriction. After you have ascertained the means which are suitable, or proper, you must go further and ascertain whether they are necessary. If they are not necessary to attain the end, although they may be good in themselves, yet you shall not use them.

We ought to construe these words in such manner as to give to each its appropriate meaning. They are not tautologous. But if we say that *"necessary"* means *convenient,* or *useful,* or *conducive to,* then it might have been totally omitted, because the word *proper,* would have conveyed the whole meaning.

It is argued, however, that if Congress is not allowed to exercise its discretion in selecting such means "as are appropriate and conducive to the end," they cannot beneficially execute the great and important powers expressly delegated to them. It is difficult to perceive how this effect would follow, when they are allowed all the means necessary for executing those powers; but if on the contrary, they are allowed to use any means, however remotely conducive to the execution of those powers, there is no limitation whatever to their authority. Thus, a power is given to them to lay and collect taxes. They pass a law to raise the sum of ten millions of dollars by a tax on land. The necessary and proper means for collecting this tax are easily and directly within their reach, and indisputably adequate to execute the power; but this does not satisfy them. It would be extremely *convenient* and a very *appropriate* measure, and very *conducivo to* their purpose of collecting this tax speedily and promptly, if the state governments could be prohibited during the same year from laying and collecting a land tax. Were they to pass such a law, and thereby directly encroach on one of the most undoubted rights of the states, the present liberal and sweeping construction of the clause by the supreme court would justify the measure. It may be said however that this supposes an extreme case, and that we ought not to argue from the abuse of a power; that we ought not to admit that our own representatives will so egregiously betray their solemn trusts. To this remark I would answer, that a fair conclusion drawn from your premises ought not to be opposed by the application of *"the magic word confidence."* I cannot exclusively rely on my confidence in our representatives: if that were a sufficient guarantee for the preservation of our state rights, then there would be no necessity for a specific enumeration of granted powers.

It is contended by the supreme court, that if the word *necessary* is restricted in its signification, to those means alone without which the powers given would be nugatory, its application to any of the powers of the government will be found so pernicious in its operation that we shall be compelled to discard it. This assertion is supported by reference to sundry examples. It is said that "the whole penal code of the United States rests on implication; that the power of punishing offences is not to be found among the enumerated powers of government, except in two instances; and that the several powers of government might exist, altho' in a very imperfect state, and be carried into execution, although no punishment should be inflicted in cases when the right to punish is not expressly given." The ready answer to these positions is that the power of punishment is a natural and *necessary* incident to the power of making laws: if the power to make the rule be given, the power of enforcing its observance is a *necessary* incident to that power. A law without its appropriate sanction is an absurdity in terms: It is no law, but a recommendation only. One example referred to by the court is the power "to establish post offices and post roads." It is said that this power is executed by the single act of making the establishment; that the right to carry the mail, and to punish the mail robber, have been inferred from it, and that those rights are not indispensably *necessary* to the establishment of a post office and post road. In this conclusion I certainly do not concur. Without the right to carry the mail, the post office, and post roads would not be established. The right to carry the mail is not an implied power, but one which is involved in the very power to establish the office *to which* the mail is to be carried, and the roads, *along which* it is to travel. The right to punish the mail robber is incidental, and is implied *necessarily* from the power to carry the mail.—So, too, the power of punishing the crimes of falsifying records, &c. and of perjuries, is a *necessary* power to the administration of justice by the courts of the U. States; because the administration of justice *could not* be carried on, if these crimes could be perpetrated with impunity. With respect to the other example quoted by the chief justice, there is at the first view some difficulty, but when we examine it more critically the difficulty vanishes. He says that there is only one oath prescribed by the constitution, namely, the oath to support it; that the powers vested in congress can all be executed without requiring any other oath; but that congress have imposed the oath of office, and that no one has yet doubted their power to require such an oath, or any other that their wisdom might suggest. In reply to this remark, I would ask, why congress or any other legislative body have been in the habit of passing laws requiring this sanction. Because the infirmity of human nature has been supposed to require it, or in other words, to render it *necessary*; because it has been believed that with respect to mankind in general, it is deemed indispensable that the existence of God, the dispenser of rewards and punishments in a future life, should always be present to the mind of the man who is called on to give testimony in a court of justice, or to execute any important official function. Let us not then be told at this day "that the power to exact this security for the faithful performance of duty is not indispensably necessary." That remark might well be made by some youthful theorist, by some Utopian, or Godwinian speculator, but proceeds with a very bad grace from the lips of the sage judges of the land. The practical politicians of Europe and America all concur in requiring oaths as a necessary sanction for the performance of official duties; Paley and all the most approved moralists inculcate the *necessity* of them. It is therefore perfectly clear that the requisition of an oath is within the constitutional powers of Congress.

If the examples, which the chief justice has thus chosen for the purpose of shewing that the restricted sense of the term *"necessary"* would be found pernicious in its operation, be the strongest examples that can be put (and who will doubt it, as *he* has chosen them?) I think it follows inevitably that we shall not be obliged to discard it.

It had been frequently asserted during the debates on the constitution, and before its adoption, that this clause was in reality no grant of power, that it conveyed nothing but what would have resulted to the government by unavoidable implication. "No axiom is more clearly established in law," says the Federalist, No. 44, "than that wherever a general power to do a thing is given, every particular power *necessary* for doing it is included."* This maxim is well expressed by the antient authors of the English law. *"Quando lex aliquid alicui concedit, concedere videtur et id,* SINE QUO *res ipsa esse non potest."* When the law grants any thing to a person, it also gives that *without which* the thing itself cannot be. Or as Lord Coke interprets it, "when the law doth give any thing to one, it giveth impliedly whatsoever is *necessary* for the taking and enjoying the same." Thus "when lands are let by one man to another at the will of the lessor and the lessee sows the land, and the lessor after it is sown, and before the corn is ripe, put him out, yet the lessee shall have the corn, and *shall have free entry, egress,*

---

* See also one of George Nicholas's speeches in convention, and other speeches.

and regress to cut and carry away the corn." [Coke Litt. 56.] This Latin maxim affords the best definition of what is meant by necessary means. They are those means *without which* the end *could not* be attained. The clause then conveys no grant of powers; it was inserted from abundant caution, or perhaps for the purpose of letting in the power contained in the latter part of the clause, and of vesting in the legislature rather than the other departments the power of making laws to carry into effect the "other powers vested in the government, or *in any department or officer thereof.*" Let us then suppose that this clause had not been inserted. Congress then would have had a right to use the means *necessary* to effectuate their granted powers, and no more; they could only have used those means *sine quo* (without which) their express powers could not have been carried into execution. The insertion of the clause has no greater effect: it confers no new power. When a law is about to pass, the enquiry which ought to be made by Congress is, does the constitution expressly grant this power? if not, then, is this law one *without which* some power cannot be executed? If it is not, then it is a power reserved to the states, or to the people, and we may not use the means, nor pass the law.

The government of the U.S. is one of specified and limited powers. Altho' limited, they are yet ample, they are vast. It is entrusted with the regulation of all our external concerns; it is empowered to protect us from foreign nations and from internal dissentions. For this purpose it may lay taxes, borrow money, raise armies, govern the militia, build ships, and exercise every power which it is necessary should be exercised to attain those great and desirable objects. The purse and the sword are placed in its hands. The state governments have all residuary power; every thing necessary for the protection of the lives, liberty and property of individuals is left subject to their control; the contracts of every class of society, agricultural, mercantile, or mechanical, are regulated by their laws, except in those cases where uniformity was desirable, in which cases the states fully surrendered the power.

This residuary power was left in possession of the states for wise purposes. It is necessary that the laws which regulate the daily transactions of men should have a regard to their interests, their feelings, even their prejudices. This can better be done when the territory is of moderate dimensions, than when it is immense; it is more peculiarly proper too in the situation of our society, where we have been always accustomed to our own laws, and our own legislatures, and where the laws of one state will not suit the people of another; it is still more important that this division of legislative power into external and internal should be rigidly adhered to, and its proper distribution religiously observed, when we reflect that the accumulation of these powers into the hands of one government would render it too strong for the liberty of the people, and would inevitably erect a throne upon the ruins of the republic. Why then should the federal government grasp at powers not necessary for carrying into effect their acknowledged powers? why should they trench upon those interior measures which were reserved by the states for their own regulation and controul? why should they so eagerly, year after year, and session after session, encroach upon state rights, and make one encroachment a precedent for another? or why should they assume even doubtful powers, when they are vested with so many undoubted powers perfectly adequate for all their legitimate purposes?

I think it clear that the intention of the constitution was to confer on Congress the power of resorting to such means as are incidental to the express powers; to such means as directly and necessarily tend to produce the desired effect. If the chief or principal object of the instrument intended to be used, be such as to produce other effects, or to conduce to some other end, it cannot be considered as a necessary instrument for effectuating the desired end, although it may remotely have a tendency to produce the desired effect. Thus, a bank is principally intended to benefit individual merchants and traders: it is said to increase their capitals, or at any rate to enable them, by means of the credit which they acquire by

banking operations, to push their mercantile dealings and specu-
lations farther than they could do without that aid: true, after
they are established, they may afford some facilities to the government in collecting and distributing their taxes, and may sometimes
enable it to borrow money—but, that is not the chief object of their
institution; nor would that advantage ever accrue to a government from the institution, unless through the medium of the bene-
fits rendered to individuals. But laws incorporating banks for the
benefit of individuals, fall naturally and properly within the jurisdiction of the state governments. Those governments regulate
the internal affairs of the people, and banks not being *necessary* to
enable the federal government either to collect its taxes, or to borrow money, their incorporation seems not to have been intended
to be given, and therefore was reserved to the states.

It may however be asked, whether I can at this day pretend to
argue against the constitutionality of a bank established by Congress. In answer, I reply, that it is not my intention by these
remarks to bring that subject into discussion. I am willing to
acquiesce in that particular case, so long as the charter continues
without being violated—because it has been repeatedly argued
before Congress, and not only in 1791, but in 1815 was solemnly
decided in favor of the measure. But it is against the *principles*
which brought it into life in the year 1791, and those by which it
is supported now by the supreme court, that I protest: I deprecate
the consequences of those principles, and wish to raise my feeble
voice in warning my countrymen of the danger of them. There
is supposed to have been a very wide difference between the principles which caused that bank to be established in 1791, and those
of 1815. On the first occasion it was boldly urged by Mr. Hamilton, that *"necessary"* meant *useful, or conducive to*; that the bank,
although not indispensably necessary, would be convenient, and
would facilitate the collection of the revenue, and the borrowing
of money; and the preamble to the bank bill recited that "it is
conceived to be *conducive* to the successful conducting of the

finances, and conceived to *tend* to give facility to the obtaining of loans." The reason however which prevailed in 1815 was different. It was then conceived that the establishment of a bank was a *necessary* means for conducting the fiscal operations of the government; it was urged with great warmth that the government could not go on without it. Altho' in 1811 the charter of the old bank expired, there could not be found friends enough to renew it; but in 1815 the paper which had been thrown into circulation by the establishment of numerous state banks, having become extremely depreciated, and the commerce of the country having become thereby very much embarrassed, many members of Congress began to believe that the only cure for the evil was the establishment of a national bank. It was believed by some, that, without it, the revenue could neither be collected nor distributed. They thought that the necessity which the constitution required was now apparent, and under the influence of this opinion, a majority was obtained, and the measure was (I think unfortunately), ushered into existence. Under the influence of this opinion, and perhaps under a belief that the long acquiescence of the people under a bank law justified it, the President, Madison, approved of the bill, notwithstanding his former hostility to such a law. Subsequent events have rendered it extremely doubtful whether any benefit will result from it. This change of opinion is however referred to in the opinion of the supreme court, and is arrayed with great force against the opponents of the measure. The reference to that change of opinion shews how extremely cautious we ought to be in admitting an enlarged construction of the powers given to Congress, since this very admission has been wielded with great force; and there is every reason to believe that it will in future cases be used as a wedge whereby to let in other powers of indefinite extent, and inconceivable capacity.

The consequences of giving an enlarged, or what is called a liberal construction to the grant of powers, are alarming to the states and the people. The disposition to give this enlarged construction has manifested itself on many occasions, and particularly during the short and eventful period of Mr. Adams's administration.—Whilst this disposition exists, unchecked and uncontrolled, the first clause of the 8th section is big with dangers. "Congress shall have power to lay and collect taxes, &c. to pay the debts, and provide for the common defence and *general welfare* of the U.S." Whilst the constitution was under discussion, its opponents foretold that this clause would be construed into an unlimited commission to exercise every power, which might be alleged to be necessary to the general welfare. The Federalist (No. 41) treated that prophecy with contempt. He asked, "For what purpose could the enumeration of particular powers be inserted, if these and all others were meant to be included in the preceding general power?" Notwithstanding the opinion of the Federalist, the prophecy of the opponents of the constitution turned out to be true. It was contended by some, that congress had a right to pass any law by which they might "provide for the general welfare," and they brought in the preamble to their aid; whilst others only claimed the privilege of providing for the general welfare in ALL cases in which there might be an application of the money to be raised by taxes. In this latter sense it was understood by the first secretary of the treasury, who maintained that there was "no room for doubt that whatever concerns the general interests of learning, of agriculture, of manufactures and of commerce, are within the sphere of the national councils, as far as regards an application of money." The effect of either of these constructions is to render nugatory the particular enumeration of powers. There was no necessity for a specific enumeration of authorities, the execution of which required the raising of money by taxes, and the expenditure thereof, if the general phrase authorized the Congress to pass laws in all cases in which the expenditure of money might promote the general welfare.

This liberal disposition for granting power is unhappily sanctioned by the late decision of the supreme court. I dread the result.

Take the two clauses together, construe them liberally, and point out, if you can, the limit which may be assigned to the exercise of their powers.

They may lay out their money on roads and canals; they may grant writs of ad quod damnum to condemn the land on which the road may pass, and finding that the object could be better attained and the money more judiciously applied by corporate bodies than by their own agents, they may create boards for internal improvement.

They may build universities, academies, and school houses for the poor, and incorporate companies for the better management thereof.

They may incorporate companies for the promotion of agriculture, and vest in those companies a portion of their own funds in order to contribute to the general welfare.

They may build churches, because it promotes the general welfare of the people, to resort to places of public worship, and they may support from the treasury those ministers of the gospel, whose tenets may in their opinion best advance the general welfare, that is, conduce to the strength of the government.

When consequences such as these are plainly deducible from the enlarged construction of the constitution, we must without hesitation pronounce that such construction is inadmissible.

The supreme court have remarked that there may be cases in which "it would become the painful duty of that tribunal to say that an act of Congress was not the law of the land." I apprehend this can hardly ever be the case, where the act is one which gives power to the federal government. The latitude of their construction will render it unnecessary for them to discharge a duty *so* "painful" to their feelings. Every dollar of which Congress authorizes the expenditure, and every power which they assume, will contribute in some way or other, "to promote the general welfare," or at least will be an useful, or convenient instrument, or will "conduce to" some good end which they may have in view.

Congress too, are the sole judges of the *necessity*, that is, the convenience of any instrument, and to attempt to control their discretion, would be treading on legislative ground.

The safety of the states will be found in their own firmness, their own vigilance, and their own wisdom.

I will make no remarks on the second question decided by the supreme court.

If the Bank law be constitutional, or if it be acquiesced in as such, it seems to follow that the states cannot forbid the establishment of one in their territory, nor expel it; and I think the conclusion drawn by the court is at least feasible, that it cannot be taxed.* The same course of reasoning however, which would prove that the states cannot tax the bank, or other institutions established by Congress, would also prove that the Congress cannot tax the banks or other institutions established by the states.

The principal satisfactory reason why the states cannot tax an institution of the United States is, that the power of taxation involves the power of destruction; and that "one government has not a right to pull down, where there is an acknowledged right in another to build up; nor a right in one government to destroy where there is a right in another to preserve."

Now it is admitted that the states have an undisputed right to incorporate companies for all purposes whatsoever. That right is reserved to them in its fullest latitude. If the United States can tax the operations of a state bank, or of a canal company, or any other company established by a state, they may tax it so high as to destroy it altogether; and it would be impossible for any state institution to continue its operations without the approbation or permission of Congress. Such a result would destroy the sovereignty of the states within that very sphere in which it is admitted they may act without control: it would render them subordinate

---

* On this proposition however I have not bestowed much reflection, and should be glad to see the arguments of the counsel for the State of Maryland on it.

in every thing. If then, the undisputed right of the states to lay taxes be limited by the constitutional right of Congress to create certain institutions, such as custom houses, post offices, the mint, &c.—it necessarily follows that the right of Congress to lay taxes is also limited by the right of the states to erect banking institutions, or any other corporation. If the governments are to move on harmoniously, neither ought to attempt to pull down what the other has a *right* to build up. And this duty is as imperative on the government of the U. States, as it is on those of the several states.

The conduct of our own state upon the subject of taxing the Bank of the United States is worthy of praise. The legislature of Virginia have always been of opinion that Congress had no right to establish a bank. They have remonstrated against the exercise of the power; they instructed their senators to vote against the measure, and most of our representatives have uniformly been opposed to it. Yet in Virginia no tax has been laid on the operations of the bank. Her course is more wise. When unconstitutional laws are passed, this state calmly passes her resolutions to that effect; she endeavors to convince the public mind of the baneful effects of usurped powers; she endeavors to unite and combine the moral force of the states against usurpation, and she never will employ force to support her doctrines, till other measures have entirely failed. May this continue to be her policy, and may the other states follow her example! I do most ardently hope that this decision of the supreme court will attract the attention of the state legislatures, and that Virginia will, as heretofore, do her duty.

April 2, 1819   AMPHICTYON

Marshall's "A Friend to the Union" Essays

Philadelphia *Union*, April 24–28, 1819

I

Mr. Editor:

My attention has been a good deal attracted by some essays which have appeared lately in one of the Virginia papers which seem to have for their object the infliction of deep wounds on the constitution through a misrepresentation of the opinion lately delivered by the Supreme Court on the constitutionality of the act incorporating the bank of the United States. I have bestowed a few leisure moments on the refutation of some of the mischievous errours contained in these essays; and, if you think what I have written worth publishing you will give this answer to Amphyction a place in your useful paper.

A spirit which was supposed to have been tranquillized by a long possession of the government, appears to be resuming its original activity in Virginia. The decision of the Supreme Court in the case of McCullough against the state of Maryland has been seized as a fair occasion for once more agitating the publick mind, and reviving those unfounded jealousies by whose blind aid ambition climbs the ladder of power.

The bill for incorporating a bank of the United States had become a law, without exciting a single murmur. The reason is obvious. Those who fill the legislative and executive departments are elected by the people, and are of course popular. In addition, they possess great power and great patronage. Had they been unjustly attacked, champions would have arisen on every side, who would with equal zeal and ability have presented the truth to a publick not unwilling to perceive it. But the Judges of the

Supreme Court, separated from the people by the tenure of office, by age, and by the nature of their duties, are viewed with respect, unmingled with affection, or interest. They possess neither power nor patronage. They have no sops to give; and every coffeehouse furnishes a Cerberus, hoping some reward for that watchfulness which his bark proclaims; and restrained by no apprehension that any can be stimulated by personal considerations to expose the injustice of his attacks. We ought not, therefore, to be surprised if it should be deemed criminal in the judicial department to sustain a measure, which was adopted by the legislature, and by the executive with impunity. Hostility to the Union, must cease to be guided by its usual skill, when it fails to select the weakest department as that through which a breach may be effected.

The Inquirer, the leading paper of Virginia, abounds with hostile attacks on this opinion. That which is written with most talent, most system, and most design, appears under the signature of Amphyction. The Editor assures his readers that it contains "a most satisfactory exposition" "of the alarming errours of the Supreme Court of the United States" in their interpretation of the constitution; and Amphyction himself does not leave his object to conjecture. "Most ardently" does he "hope that this decision of the Supreme Court will attract the attention of the state legislatures, and that Virginia will, as heretofore, do her duty."

The avowed object being of so serious a nature, it behoves not only the friends of the Bank, but the friends of the constitution, the friends of Union, to examine well the principles which are denounced as heretical, and those which are supported as orthodox.

The objections of Amphyction are to that part of the opinion which declares the act incorporating the bank to be constitutional. He introduces them with expressing his disapprobation of that mode of transacting their official duties which the Supreme Court has adopted. He would prefer *seriatim* opinions, to the combined opinion of the bench delivered by a single Judge.

On the justness of this criticism in general, or on its peculiar application to this particular case, I shall make no observation; because the principles expressed in this single opinion are neither more nor less vulnerable than they would have been if expressed in six separate opinions. But the criticism was made for the purpose of conveying an insinuation which marks the spirit in which the discussion is conducted. "We are not," says Amphyction, "informed whether the whole court united in the course of reasoning adopted by the Chief Justice, nor whether they all accorded in the various positions and principles he advanced."

Now I humbly conceive this is a subject on which we are informed. The opinion is delivered, not in the name of the chief justice, but in the name of the whole court. This observation applies to the "reasoning adopted," and "to the various positions and principles which were advanced" as entirely as to the conclusions drawn from "those positions and principles." Throughout the whole opinion, the chief justice never speaks in the singular number, or in his own person, but as the mere organ of the court. In the presence of all the judges, and in their names he advances certain propositions as their propositions, and certain reasoning as their reasoning. I appeal to Amphyction himself, I appeal to every man accustomed to judicial proceedings, to determine whether the judges of the Supreme Court, men of high and respectable character, would sit by in silence, while great constitutional principles of which they disapproved, were advanced in their name, and as their principles. I appeal to the usage of the Supreme Court itself. Their decisions are reported, and are in possession of the publick. It has often happened that a judge concurring in the opinion of the court, but on reasons peculiar to himself, has stated his own reasoning. The great case of the Nereid is one among many examples, of this course of proceeding. In some instances too it has occurred, that the judge delivering the opinion of the court, has stated the contrariety of reasoning on which the opinion was formed. Of this, the case of Olivera v. the Union Ensurance Co. is an example. The course of every tribunal must necessarily be, that the opinion which is to be delivered as the opinion of the court, is previously submitted to the consideration of all the judges; and, if any part of the reasoning be disapproved, it must be so modified as to receive the approbation of all, before it can be delivered as the opinion of all. Amphyction himself thinks so; for he says: "We are driven, however reluctantly, to the conclusion that each judge approves of each argument and position advanced by the chief justice."

Why then has he suggested a contrary idea? He leaves us in no uncertainty for the answer to this question.

After stating that the subject is one "which has employed his (the chief justice's) thoughts, his tongue, and his pen, as a politician and as an historian for more than thirty years," he adds that it "is one which has, perhaps more than any other, heretofore drawn a broad line of distinction between the two great parties in this country, in which line no one has taken a more distinguished and decided rank than the judge who has thus expounded the supreme law of the land."

The chief justice then is a federalist; who was a politician of some note before he was a judge; and who with his tongue and his pen, supported the opinions he avowed. To expose the reasoning of the court to still greater odium, if it be possible, we are told that "the liberal and latitudinous construction" he has attached to a term in the constitution, had been attached to it before him, "by Mr. Secretary Hamilton." The reasoning, then, of the court is, dexterously enough, ascribed to Mr. Secretary Hamilton and the chief justice, two inveterate federalists. This question cannot be trusted, by Amphyction, to his exposition of the constitution, unless the spirit of party be introduced into the cause, and made its judge. How favourable this spirit is to truth, and to a fair exercise of the human judgement, Amphyction well knows. Had he admitted this opinion, including the reasoning, to be what it professes to be,—what it must be,—the opinion and the reasoning of all the judges,—four of whom have no political sin upon their heads;—who in addition to being eminent lawyers, have the still greater advantage of being sound republicans; of having been selected certainly not for their federalism, by Mr. Jefferson, and Mr. Madison, for the high stations they so properly fill, his argument would have been stripped of one powerful recommendation, and must have depended rather more on its intrinsick merit. We need not then be surprised that this improbable suggestion is made, although a sense of propriety has compelled the writer to abandon it as soon as its effect was produced.

Having thus prepared his readers for the dangerous errours contained in the opinion of the Supreme Court, Amphyction proceeds to inform them what those errours are.

"The first is the denial that the powers of the federal government were delegated by the states; and the second is that the grant of powers to that government, and particularly the grant of powers *necessary and proper* to carry the other powers into effect, ought to be construed in a liberal rather than a restricted sense."

But before Amphyction can permit himself to enter on his first point, he deems it necessary to cast a little more odium on the opinion he is about to examine. "For what purpose," he asks, "did the federal court decide that question?" After stating that it was totally unnecessary, that the opinion on it "is obiter and extra-judicial;" he adds that "whether the powers of the federal government were delegated to it by the states in their sovereign capacity, or by the people, can make but little difference in the extent of those powers. In either case it is still true that the powers of that government are limited by the charter that called it into existence" &c.

I shall not controvert the proposition that the constitution ought to receive the same construction, whether its powers were delegated by the people or the states. That Amphyction entertains the same opinion, is brought into some doubt by the extreme importance he attaches to his theory.

If the powers of the general government were to be in no degree affected by the source from which they were derived, it is not easy to comprehend how the liberty of the American people can depend on the adoption of the one opinion or of the other. The origin of the government would seem to be a mere historical fact, which it would be desirable to settle correctly, but for the settlement of which it could scarcely be necessary to call on the legislatures of the respective states, or to express so earnest a hope that "Virginia would, as usual, do her duty." If it be possible for Amphyction to persuade himself that the right of the state legislatures "to canvass" or "remonstrate against the publick measures of the Congress or of the President," depended on their having delegated to the general government all its powers, it would prove only with what facility the most intelligent mind may impose on itself, when pursuing a favourite and dominant idea. Surely nothing can be more obvious, nothing better established, than that the right to canvass the measures of government, or to remonstrate against the abuse of power, must reside in all who are affected by those measures, or over whom that power is exercised, whether it was delegated by them or not. Were this allegation of Amphyction true, it would follow that the people have no right to canvass the measures of government, or to remonstrate against them. The right to canvass and remonstrate resides, according to his argument, in those only who have delegated the powers of the government. Those powers were delegated, not by the people, but by the states in their sovereign capacity. It follows that the states in their sovereign capacity, not the people, have the right to canvass publick measures. If this conclusion be false, as it must be, the premises are false also; and that a man of Amphyction's intelligence should have advanced them, only proves that he is too little accustomed to political opposition, and is too confident of the prejudices he addresses, to be very attentive to the correctness of his positions, or to the accuracy of his reasoning.

But if Amphyction had not been more anxious to throw obloquy on the court than to ascertain its justice, he might have spared this unnecessary charge of travelling out of the case for the purpose of delivering, extrajudicially, a doctrine so dangerous as he represents this to be. The principles he now maintains, appear to have been advanced, and relied on at the bar. "The counsel for the state of Maryland," we are told in the opinion, "have deemed it of some importance in the construction of the constitution to consider that instrument, not as emanating from the people; but, as the act of sovereign and independent states. The powers of the general government, it has been said, are delegated by the states who alone are truly sovereign, and must be exercised in subordination to the states, who alone possess supreme dominion." It is in consequence of this argument that the subject is introduced into the opinion.

His eagerness to censure must be much stronger than his sense of justice, who will criminate a court for noticing an argument advanced by eminent counsel, as one of leading importance in the cause.

But waiving any further discussion of these incidental observations, I will proceed to consider the first objection made to the opinion of the Supreme Court. It is stated to be "the denial that the powers of the federal government were delegated by the states."

This assertion is not literally true.—The court has not, in terms, denied "that the powers of the federal government were delegated by the states," but has asserted affirmatively that it "is emphatically and truly a government of the people," that it "in form and in substance emanates from them."

If Amphyction chuses to construe the affirmative assertion made by the court into a negative assertion that "the powers of the government were not delegated by the states," I shall not contest the point with him unless he uses the word "states" in a different sense from that which a great part of his argument imports. In what sense, let me ask, does he use the word? Does he mean the people inhabiting that territory which constitutes a state? Or does he mean the government of that territory? If the former, the controversy is at an end. He concurs with the opinion he arraigns. The Supreme Court cannot be mistaken. It has said, not indeed in the same words, but in substance, precisely what he says. The powers of the government were delegated, according to that opinion, by the people assembled in convention in their respective states, and deciding, as all admit, for their respective states.

If Amphyction means to assert, as I suppose he does, that the powers of the general government were delegated by the state legislatures, then I say that his assertion is contradicted by the words of the constitution, and by the fact; and is not supported even by that report, on which he so confidently relies.

The words of an instrument, unless there be some sinister design which shuns the light, will always represent the intention of those who frame it. An instrument intended to be the act of the people, will purport to be the act of the people. An instrument intended to be the act of the states, will purport to be the act of the states. Let us then examine those words of the constitution, which designate the source whence its powers are derived. They are: "We the people of the United States, in order to form a more perfect union, &c. do ordain and establish this constitution for the United States of America."

The constitution then proceeds in the name of the people to define the powers of that government which they were about to create.

This language cannot be misunderstood. It cannot be construed to mean, "We the states, &c."

If still more complete demonstration on this point could be required, it will be furnished by a comparison of the words just recited from the constitution, with those used in the articles of confederation.

The confederation was intended to be the act of the states, and was drawn in language comporting with that intention. The style is: "Articles of confederation and perpetual union between the states of New Hampshire, Massachusetts Bay, &c." The 3d article is completely descriptive of the character of the instrument. It is in these words: "The said states hereby severally enter into a firm league of friendship with each other for their common defence, the security of their liberties, and their mutual and general welfare; binding themselves to assist each other against all force offered to, or attacks made upon them, or any of them, on account of religion, sovereignty, trade, or any other pretence whatever."

The confederation was a mere alliance offensive and defensive, and purports to be, what it was intended to be,—the act of sovereign states. The constitution is a government acting on the people, and purports to be, what it was intended to be,—the act of the people.

The fact itself is in perfect consonance with the language of the instrument. It was not intended to submit the constitution to the decision of the state legislatures, nor was it submitted to their decision. It was referred to conventions of the people "for their assent or ratification," whose decision thereon was not to be reported to the state legislatures but to Congress. Had the legislature of every state in the Union been hostile to the constitution, it would still have gone into operation, if assented to and ratified by the conventions of the people. With what propriety, then, can it be denied to be the act of the people?

On this part of the question also, a comparison with the mode of proceeding for the adoption of the constitution, which was the act of the people, with that observed in adopting the confederation, which was the act of the states, may not be altogether useless.

We have seen that the constitution was submitted to the people themselves assembled in convention.

The confederation was submitted to the state legislatures, who adopted or rejected it; and who expressed their adoption by empowering their members in Congress, who were their ministers plenipotentiary, to subscribe it in their behalf.

I cannot be mistaken when I say that no political proposition was ever more fully demonstrated than that maintained by the Supreme Court of the United States, respecting the source from which the government of the Union derives its powers.

I will now show that the very report cited by Amphyction admits the proposition contained in the opinion he reprobates.

Certain resolutions he informs us had been adopted by the legislature of Virginia in 1798, one of which contained the assertion that the assembly viewed "the powers of the federal government as resulting from the compact to which the states are parties." "Those resolutions," he says, "having been disapproved of by most of the other state legislatures, became the subject of examination at the succeeding session, and produced that remarkable commentary which has generally been known by the name of Madison's report." The language of this commentary on this part of the resolution is: "It is indeed true that the term 'states,' is sometimes used in a vague sense and sometimes in different senses, according to the subject to which it is applied. Thus it sometimes means the separate sections of territory occupied by the political societies within each; sometimes the particular governments established by those societies; sometimes those societies as organized into those particular governments; and lastly, it means the people in their highest sovereign capacity."

In which of these senses does the committee assert that the states are parties to the constitution or compact? In that sense in which the term is used to designate the government established by the particular society within the territory? No. The chairman of that committee had too much self respect, too much respect for the opinions of intelligent men out of Virginia as well as in it, to advance a proposition so totally untrue. The report continues: "Whatever different constructions of the term 'states' in the resolution may have been entertained, all will at least concur in that last mentioned" (the people composing those political societies in their highest sovereign capacity) "because," the report proceeds, "in that sense the constitution was submitted to the 'states.'

In that sense the states ratified it; and in that sense they are consequently parties to the compact from which the powers of the federal government result."

This celebrated report, then, concurs exactly with the Supreme court, in the opinion that the constitution is the act of the people.

I will now examine the facts on which those arguments are founded, with which Amphyction attempts to support his most extraordinary dogma.

The first is that "the federal convention of 1787, was composed of delegates appointed by the respective state legislatures."

This fact is stated in the opinion of the court; and the inference drawn from it is completely refuted by the observation that the constitution, when it came from the hands of that convention, was a mere proposal without any obligation. Its whole obligation is derived from the assent and ratification of the people afterwards assembled in state conventions. Had Amphyction confined himself to the assertion that the constitution was proposed to the people by delegates appointed by the state legislatures, he would have accorded with the Supreme Court, and would have asserted a fact which I believe no person is disposed to deny.

His second proposition is: "That the constitution was submitted to conventions elected by the people of the several states; that is to say, to the states themselves in their highest political and sovereign authority; by those separate conventions, representing, not the whole mass of the people of the United States, but the people only within the limits of the respective sovereign states, the constitution was adopted and brought into existence. The individuality of the several states was still kept up, &c."

It surely cannot escape Amphyction himself, that these positions accord precisely with the opinion he pronounces so mischievously erroneous. He admits in terms the whole subject in controversy. He admits that the powers of the general government were not delegated by the state governments, but by the people of the respective states. This is the very proposition advanced by the Supreme Court, and advanced in terms too plain to be mistaken. The argument on the part of the state of Maryland was, as we learn from the opinion, that the constitution did not emanate from the people, but was the act of sovereign and independent states; clearly using the term "states" in a sense distinct from the term "people." It is this argument which is denied by the court; and in discussing it, after stating that the constitution was submitted to conventions of the people in their respective states, the opinion adds: "From these conventions the constitution derives its whole authority."

Were it possible to render the views of the court on this subject more clear, it is done in that part of the opinion which controverts the proposition advanced by the counsel for the state of Maryland, "that the people had already surrendered all their power to the state sovereignties and had nothing more to give;" and which, in opposition to this doctrine, maintains that the legitimacy of the general government would be much more questionable had it been created by the states. It is impossible to read that paragraph and retain a single doubt, if indeed a doubt could ever have been created, of the clear understanding of the court that the term "people" was used as designating the people of the states, and the term "states" as designating their government.

Amphyction adds, that those conventions represented "not the whole mass of the people of the United States, but the people only within the limits of the respective sovereign states." "The individuality of the several states was still kept up, &c."

And who has ever advanced the contrary opinion? Who has ever said that the convention of Pennsylvania represented the people of any other state, or decided for any other state than itself? who has ever been so absurd as to deny that "the individuality of the several states was still kept up?" Not the Supreme Court certainly. Such opinions may be imputed to the judges, by those who, finding nothing to censure in what is actually said, and being predetermined to censure, create odious phantoms which may be very proper objects of detestation, but which bear no resemblance to any thing that has proceeded from the court.

Nothing can be more obvious than that in every part of the opinion, the terms "state" and "state sovereignties" are used in reference to the state governments, as contradistinguished from the people of the states. The words of the federal convention, requesting that the constitution might "be submitted to a convention of delegates chosen in each state by the people thereof," are quoted; and it is added, "This mode of proceeding was adopted; and by the convention, by congress, and by the state legislatures, the instrument was submitted to the people." That is, to the people of the respective states; for that is the mode of proceeding said to have been recommended by the convention, and to have been adopted.—After noticing that they assembled in their respective states, the opinion adds: "And where else should they have assembled? No political dreamer was ever wild enough to think of breaking down the lines which separate the states, and of compounding the American people into one mass."

Yet Amphyction affects to be controverting the reasoning of the supreme court when he says that the convention of our state did not represent all the people of the United States, that "the individuality of the several states was still kept up." Disregarding altogether the language of the court, he ascribes to the judges an opinion which they say "no political dreamer was ever wild enough to think of."

The next proposition advanced by Amphyction is that "the President is elected by persons who are, as to numbers, partly chosen on the federal principle"; and that the senators are chosen by the state legislatures.

If these facts are alleged for the purpose of proving that the powers of the general government were delegated by the state legislatures, he has not shown us, and I confess I do not perceive, their bearing on that point. If they are alleged to prove the separate existence of the states, he has very gravely demonstrated what every body knows, & what no body denies. He would be about as usefully employed in convincing us that we see with our eyes & hear with our ears.

The last fact on which the argument of Amphyction is founded is, that the constitution is to be amended by the legislatures of three fourths of the states, or by conventions of the same number of states, in the manner provided by the 5th article.

It is not true that the legislatures of the states can of themselves amend the constitution. They can only decide on those amendments which have previously been recommended to them by Congress. Or they may require Congress to call a convention of the people to propose amendments, which shall, at the discretion of Congress, be submitted to the state legislatures, or to conventions to be assembled in the respective states.

Were it untrue that the constitution confers on the state legislatures the power of making amendments, that would not prove that this power was delegated to them by themselves. The amendments would indeed be the act of the states, but the original would still be the act of the people.

I have now reviewed the first number of Amphyction; and will only add my regrets that a gentleman whose claims to our respect appear to be by no means inconsiderable should manifest such excessive hostility to the powers necessary for the preservation of the Union, as to arraign with such bitterness the opinion of the supreme court on an interesting constitutional question, either for doctrines not to be found in it, or on principles totally repugnant to the words of the constitution, and to the recorded facts respecting its adoption.

April 24, 1819   A FRIEND TO THE UNION

II

Mr. Editor:

The second errour supposed by Amphyction to be contained in the opinion of the Supreme Court is: "That the grant of powers to Congress which may be *necessary and proper* to carry into execution, the other powers granted to them or to any department of the government, ought to be construed in a liberal rather than a restricted sense."

For the sake of accuracy I will observe that the Supreme Court has not said that this grant ought to be construed in a "liberal sense;" although it has certainly denied that it ought to be construed in that "restricted sense" for which Amphyction contends. If by the term "liberal sense" is intended an extension of the grant beyond the fair and usual import of the words, the principle is not to be found in the opinion we are examining.

There is certainly a medium between that restricted sense which confines the meaning of words to narrower limits than the common understanding of the world affixes to them, and that extended sense which would stretch them beyond their obvious import. There is a fair construction which gives to language the sense in which it is used, and interprets an instrument according to its true intention. It is this medium, this fair construction that the Supreme Court has taken for its guide. No passage can, I think, be extracted from the opinion, which recognises a different rule; and the passages are numerous which recognise this. In commenting on the omission of the word "expressly" in the 10th amendment, the court says: "Thus leaving the question whether the particular power which may become the subject of contest, has been delegated to the one government or prohibited to the other, to depend on a fair construction of the whole instrument." So too, in all the reasoning on the word "necessary," the court does not, in a single instance, claim the aid of a "latitudinous," or "liberal" construction; but relies, decidedly and confidently, on its true meaning, "taking into view the subject, the context, and the intention of the framers of the constitution."

Ought any other rule to have been adopted?

Amphyction answers this question in the affirmative. This word, he contends, and indeed all the words of the constitution, ought to be understood in a restricted sense; and for not adopting his rule, the Supreme Court has drawn upon itself his heaviest censure.

The contest, then, so far as profession goes, is between the fair sense of the words used in the constitution, and a restricted sense. The opinion professes to found itself on the fair interpretation. Amphyction professes to condemn that opinion because it ought to have adopted the restricted interpretation.

The counsel for the state of Maryland had contended that the clause authorizing Congress "to pass all laws *necessary and proper* to carry into execution" the various powers vested in the government, restrained the power which Congress would otherwise have possessed; and the reasoning of Amphyction would seem to support the same proposition.

This question is of real importance to the people of the United States. If the rule contended for would not absolutely arrest the progress of the government, it would certainly deny to those who administer it the means of executing its acknowledged powers in the manner most advantageous to those for whose benefit they were conferred.

To determine whether the one course or the other be most consistent with the constitution, and with the publick good, let the principles laid down by the counsel for the state of Maryland, as stated in the opinion of the court, and the principles of Amphyction as stated by himself, be examined, and compared with the reasoning which has been so bitterly execrated.

The counsel for the state of Maryland, as we are informed, contended that the word "necessary" limits the right of Congress to pass laws for the execution of the specifick powers granted by the constitution "to such as are indispensable, and without which the power would be nugatory, that it excludes the choice of means, and leaves Congress in each case that only which is most direct and simple."

Amphyction contends that necessary means "are those means *without which* the end *could not* be obtained." "When a law is about to pass, the inquiry," he says, "which ought to be made by Congress is, does the constitution expressly grant the power? If not, then, is this law one *without which* some power *cannot* be executed? If it is not, then it is a power reserved to the states, or to the people, and we may not use the means, nor pass the law."

With some variety of expression, the position maintained in the argument of the cause, and that maintained by Amphyction, are the same. Both contend that Congress can pass no laws to carry into execution their specifick power, but such as are *indispensably* necessary; that they can employ no means but those *without which* the end *could not* be obtained.

Let us apply this rule to some of the powers delegated to the government.

Congress has power to lay and collect taxes.

According to the opinion of the Supreme Court, Congress may exercise this power in the manner most beneficial to the people, and may adopt those regulations which are adapted to the object, and will best accomplish it. But according to Amphyction, the inquiry must always be, whether the particular regulation be one *without which* the power *could not* be executed. If the power could be executed in any other way, the law is, in his opinion, unconstitutional.

Look at our tax laws. Observe their complex and multifarious regulations. All of them, no doubt, useful and conducing directly to the end;—all of them essential to the beneficial exercise of the power. But how many may be indispensably necessary;—how many may be such that without them the tax *could not* be collected, it is probable that neither Amphyction nor myself can say. In some of the laws imposing internal taxes, the collector is directed to advertise certain places of meeting, at which certain acts are to be performed; and those who do not attend and perform those acts, are subject to an increased tax. Is this regulation indispensable to the collection of the tax? It is certainly proper and convenient; but who will deny that the tax may be collected without it?

In almost every conceivable case, there is more than one mode of accomplishing the end. Which, or is either, indispensable to that end? Congress, for example, may raise armies; but we are told they can execute this power only by those means which are indispensably necessary; those without which the army could not be raised. Is a bounty proposed? Congress must inquire whether a bounty be absolutely necessary? Whether it be possible to raise an army without it? If it be possible, the bounty, on this theory, is unconstitutional.

Undoubtedly there are other means for raising an army. Men may enlist without a bounty; and if they will not, they may be drafted. A bounty, then, according to Amphyction, is unconstitutional, because the power may be executed by a draft; and a draft is unconstitutional, because the power may be executed by a bounty.

So too, Congress may provide for calling out the militia; and this power may be executed by requisitions on the governours, by direct requisitions on the militia, or, perhaps, by receiving volunteers. According to the reasoning of Amphyction, no one of these modes can be constitutional, because no one of them is indispensably necessary.

Every case presents a choice of means. Every end may be attained by different means. Of no one of these means can it be truly said, that, *"without it,* the end *could not* be attained."

The rule then laid down by Amphyction is an impracticable, and consequently an erroneous rule.

If we examine the example he has adduced for its illustration, we shall find that, instead of sustaining, it disproves his proposition. The example is this: "Where lands are let by one man to another at the will of the lessor, and the lessor sows the land, and the lessee, after it is sown and before the corn is ripe, put him out, yet the lessor shall have the corn, and shall have *free entry, ingress, and regress, to cut, and carry away the corn.*"

The right to the crop growing on the land when the lessor determines the estate, is an incident which the law, with much justice, annexes to a tenancy at will, but is not indispensable to its existence. To this right is annexed as a necessary incident, the power of carrying away the crop. The transportation of the crop then becomes the end for which entry into the land is allowed, and the mode of transportation, the means by which that end is to be accomplished.—Has the tenant the choice of means, or can he use that mode of conveyance only without which the crop cannot be carried away? A crop may be removed by employing men only, by employing men and horses, by employing horses and cars, or by employing wagons. In some instances it may be removed by land or by water. Has the person entitled to the crop, and exercising this power of conveyance, his choice of means? or may the landlord say to him, whatever mode of conveyance he may adopt, this is not indispensably necessary; you might have conveyed away the crop by other means? Undoubtedly the person allowed to carry away his crop, would not be permitted to throw down the fences, trample the enclosed fields, and trespass at will on the landholder. But he has the choice of "appropriate" means for the removal of his property, and may use that which he thinks best.

This example then might very well have been put by the court, as an apt illustration of the rule avowed in their opinion.

The rule which Amphyction gives us, for the construction of the constitution, being obviously erroneous, let us examine that which is laid down by the Supreme Court.

The Court concludes a long course of reasoning which completely demonstrates the fallacy of the construction made by the counsel for the state of Maryland, and now adopted by Amphyction, by stating its own opinion in these words: "We think the sound construction of the constitution must allow to the national legislature that discretion with respect to the means by which the powers it confers are to be carried into execution, which will enable that body to perform the high duties assigned to it, in the manner most beneficial to the people. Let the end be legitimate, let it be within the scope of the constitution, and all means which are appropriate, which are plainly adapted to that end, which are not prohibited, but consist with the letter and spirit of the constitution, are constitutional."

To this rule of construction, unless it be itself grossly misconstrued, I can perceive no objection. I think, as the Supreme Court has thought, that it would be the proper rule, were the grant which has been the subject of so much discussion, expunged from the constitution.

It is a palpable misrepresentation of the opinion of the court to say, or to insinuate that it considers the grant of a power "to pass all laws necessary and proper for carrying into execution" the powers vested in the government, as augmenting those powers, and as one which is to be construed "latitudinously," or even "liberally."

It is to be recollected that the counsel for the state of Maryland had contended that this clause was to be construed as restraining and limiting that choice of means which the national legislature would otherwise possess. The reasoning of the court is opposed to this argument, and is concluded with this observation: "The result of the most careful and attentive consideration bestowed upon this clause is, that, if it does not enlarge, it cannot be construed to restrain the powers of congress, or to impair the right of the legislature to exercise its best judgment in the selection of measures to carry into execution the constitutional powers of the government. If no other motive for its insertion can be suggested, a sufficient one is found in the desire to remove all doubt respecting the right to legislate on that vast mass of incidental powers which must be involved in the constitution, if that instrument be not a splendid bauble."

The court then has not contended that this grant enlarges, but that it does not restrain the powers of Congress; and I believe every man who reads the opinion will admit that the demonstration of this proposition is complete. It is so complete that Amphyction himself does not venture directly to controvert the conclusion; although the whole course of his reasoning seems intended to weaken the principles from which it is drawn. His whole argument appears to be intended to prove that this clause does restrain congress in the execution of all the powers conferred by the constitution, to those "means *without which* the end *could not* be obtained." Thus converting an apparent grant of power into a limitation of power.

The court has said, and I repeat it, that the constitution and laws of the United States abound with evidence demonstrating the errour of this construction. I have already stated some instances in which this rule must be discarded; and I will now refer to others which were selected by the court, the aptness of which Amphyction denies.

I will pass over the acts requiring an oath of office, because Amphyction seems half disposed to admit there is something in that particular example, and will proceed to some of those which he pronounces totally inapplicable.

Congress possesses power "to establish post offices, and post roads." Amphyction says that the right to carry the mail, and to punish those who rob it, are necessary incidents to this power. I admit it. But who does not perceive that, in making this assertion, he abandons his own interpretation of the word "necessary" and adopts that of the supreme court? Let us apply his rule to the case. Let us suppose a bill before congress to punish those who rob the mail. The inquiry is, he says: "Does the constitution expressly grant the power?" The answer must be in the negative. There is no express power to carry the mail, nor to punish those who rob it. The member is next to ask: "Is this law one without which the power cannot be executed?"—That is, can a post office and a post road be established, without an act of Congress for the punishment of those who rob the mail? The plain common sense of every man will answer this question in the affirmative. These powers were divided under the confederation. Then the conclusion of the member must be, this right to punish those who rob the mail "is a power reserved to the states, or to the people, and we may not use the means, nor pass the law. Then the state legislature may pass laws to punish those who rob the mail, but congress cannot. Post offices and post roads may be established without such a law, and therefore the power to pass it is reserved to the states." Adopt the construction of Amphyction, and this conclusion is inevitable.

Let the question be on the right of Congress to pass an act for the punishment of those who falsify a record.

The power is to ordain and establish inferiour courts, the judges of which shall hold their offices during good behaviour, and receive as a compensation for their services, salaries which shall not be diminished during their continuance in office. The second section defines the extent of the judicial power.

Is a law to punish those who falsify a record, one without which a court cannot be established, or one without which a court cannot exercise its functions? We know that under the confederation Congress had the power to establish, and did establish certain courts, and had not the power to pass laws for the punishment of those who should falsify its records.—Unquestionably such a law is "needful," "requisite," "essential," "conducive to," the due administration of justice; but no man can say it is one without which courts cannot decide causes, or without which it is physically impossible for them to perform their functions. According to the rule of Amphyction then, such a law cannot be enacted by Congress, but may be enacted by the state legislatures.

It would be tedious to go through all the examples put by the supreme court. They are all of the same character, and show, conclusively, that the principles maintained by the counsel for the state of Maryland, and by Amphyction, would essentially change the constitution, render the government of the Union incompetent to the objects for which it was instituted, and place all its powers under the control of the state legislatures. It would, in a great measure, reinstate the old confederation.

It cannot escape any attentive observer that Amphyction's stric-

tures on the opinion of the supreme court, are founded on a total
and obvious perversion of the plain meaning of that opinion, as
well as on a misconstruction of the constitution. He occasionally
substitutes words not used by the court, and employs others,
neither in the connexion, nor in the sense, in which they are employed by the court, so as to ascribe to the opinion sentiments
which it does not merely not contain, but which it excludes. The
court does not say that the word "necessary" means whatever may
be "convenient," or "useful." And when it uses "conducive to,"
that word is associated with others plainly showing that no remote,
no distant conduciveness to the object, is in the mind of the court.

With as little remorse as the Procrustes of ancient fable
stretched and lopped limbs in order to fit travellers to his bed
does Amphyction extend and contract the meaning of words in
the constitution, and in the opinion of the court, in order to accommodate those papers to his strictures. Thus, he says, if Congress
should impose a tax on Land, "it would be extremely *convenient*,
and a very *appropriate* measure, and very *conducive* to their purpose of collecting this tax speedily, and promptly, if the state
governments could be prohibited during the same year, from
laying & collecting a land tax. Were they to pass such a law and
thereby directly encroach on one of the most undoubted rights of
the states, the present liberal and sweeping construction of the
clause by the Supreme court would justify the measure."

Now I deny that a law prohibiting the state legislatures from
imposing a land tax would be an "appropriate" means, or any
means whatever, to be employed in collecting the tax of the
United States. It is not an instrument to be so employed. It is
not a means "plainly adapted," or "conducive to" the end. The
passage of such an act would be an attempt on the part of Congress, "under the pretext of executing its powers, to pass laws for
the accomplishment of objects not intrusted to the government."
So far is the construction given to this clause by the supreme court
from being so "liberal & sweeping" as to "justify the measure"

that the opinion expressly rejects it. Let its language be quoted. "That the power of taxation is one of vital importance; that it is retained by the states; that it is to be concurrently exercised by the two governments, are truths," says the opinion, "which have never been denied." The court afterwards quotes a passage from the Federalist in which this construction is urged vehemently as an objection to the constitution itself, and obviously approves the argument against it.

Many laborious criticisms would be avoided; if those who are disposed to condemn a paper, would take the trouble to read, with a disposition to understand, it.

I shall not notice the various imaginary and loose opinions which Amphyction has collected, or suggested, because they are not imputable to the supreme court. I content myself with exposing *some* errours in construing the constitution, and in ascribing to the opinion he condemns, doctrines which it does not contain.

I cannot however avoid remarking that Amphyction himself, as soon as he has closed his stricture on the supreme court, seems to desert his own construction and take up theirs. "I think it clear," he says, "that the intention of the constitution was to confer on Congress the power of resorting to such means as are incidental to the express powers; to such means as directly and necessarily tend to produce the desired effect."

How much more, let me ask, has been said by the supreme court? That court has said: "Let the end be legitimate, let it be within the scope of the constitution, and all means which are appropriate, which are plainly adapted to that end, which are not prohibited," "are constitutional." The word "appropriate," if Johnson be authority, means "peculiar," "consigned to some particular use or person,"—"belonging peculiarly."

Let the constructive words used by the supreme court, in this their acknowledged sense, be applied to any of the powers of Congress. Take for example, that of raising armies. The court has said that "all means which are appropriate," that is, "all means which are peculiar" to raising armies, which are "consigned to that particular use," which "belong peculiarly" to it, all means which are "plainly adapted" to the end, are constitutional.

If Amphyction is better pleased with his own language, I shall not contest his right to the preference; but what essential difference is there between "means which directly and necessarily tend to produce the desired effect," and means which "belong peculiarly" to the production of that effect? I acknowledge that I perceive none. Means which are "appropriate," which are "plainly adapted" to the end, must "directly and necessarily tend to produce" it. The difference however between these means, and those *without which* the effect *cannot* be produced, must be discerned by the most careless observer.

Let us apply these different definitions of the words, to any of the most common affairs of human life. A leases to B a mill for a number of years on a contract that A shall receive half the profits, and shall pay half the expenses of all the machinery which B may erect therein, and which shall be *"necessary and proper"* for the manufacture of flower. Pending this lease, the elevator and hopper boy are invented, and applied, with great advantage, to the manufacture of flower. B erects them in his mill. A is very well satisfied with receiving the increased profits, but is unwilling to pay half the expense of the machinery, because, as he alleges, it was not *"necessary"* to the manufacture of flower. All will admit that this machinery is "appropriate, and plainly adapted to the end;" or, in the words of Amphyction, that it "directly and necessarily tends to produce the desired effect." But none can think it so indispensably necessary that the end *cannot* be produced *without* it. The end was produced, flower was manufactured, before the elevator and hopper boy were invented.

The same may be observed of the cotton machine of the south, of the use of Gypsum on a farm, of many things which occur in the ordinary transactions of human life.

It will be readily perceived in every case, that this rule of construction, which seems to have escaped Amphyction in a moment when the particular object of his essay was out of view, and that contained in the opinion he condemns, are precisely the same; and are both in direct opposition to that other restricted rule by which he tries the reasoning of the supreme court.

If, as I think all will admit, that construction of the words in which Amphyction and the court concur, furnish the true rule for construing the words *"necessary and proper"* in a contract between man & man, how much more certainly must it be the true rule for construing a constitution,—an instrument the nature of which excludes the possibility of inserting in it an enumeration of the means for executing its specifick powers. If this rule be applicable to the relations between individuals, how much more applicable must it be to the relations between the people and their representatives, who are elected for the very purpose of selecting the best means of executing the powers of the government they are chosen to administer.

I have confined my observations to the reasoning of the Supreme Court, and have taken no notice of the conclusion drawn from it, because the essays I am reviewing make no objections to the latter, but denounce the former as false and dangerous. I think, on the contrary, I hazard nothing when I assert that the reasoning is less doubtful than the conclusion. I myself concur in the conclusion; but I do not fear contradiction from any fair minded and intelligent man when I say that the principles laid down by the court for the construction of the constitution may all be sound, and yet the act for incorporating the Bank be unconstitutional. But if the act be constitutional, the principles laid down by the court must be sound. I defy Amphyction, I defy any man, to furnish an argument which shall, at the same time, prove the Bank to be constitutional, and the reasoning of the court to be erroneous. Why then is Amphyction so delicate on the constitutionality of the law, while he is vehement and strenuous in his exertions to rouse the nation against the court? If we do not account for this by saying that the court is less popular, and therefore more vulnerable, than the executive and legislature, how shall we account for it?

Before I conclude let me ask this gentleman and those who think with him, what train of reasoning would have satisfied him and them? The court did not volunteer in this business. The question was brought before them, and they could not escape it. What course then does Amphyction think they ought to have adopted? Does he think they ought to have declared the law unconstitutional and void? He does not say so; and we are not permitted to draw this inference from what he does say. After lamenting that *seriatim* opinions were not delivered, he supposes what might have been the opinions of Judges concurring in the decision, but dissenting from the reasoning, delivered by the Chief Justice. "Some of them" he says, "may have believed that it was for Congress to have judged of that necessity and propriety, and having exercised their undoubted functions in so deciding, that it was not consistent with judicial modesty to say there was no such necessity, and thus to arrogate to themselves a right of putting their *veto* upon a law."

Again, he says: "It may however be asked, whether I can at this day pretend to argue against the constitutionality of a bank established by Congress? In answer, I reply that it is not my intention by these remarks to bring that subject into discussion. I am willing to acquiesce in this particular case, so long as the charter continues without being violated—because it has been repeatedly argued before Congress, and not only in 1791, but in 1815, was solemnly decided in favour of the measure."

Let us suppose that the court had supported its decision by the reasoning which Amphyction conjectures may have influenced some of the Judges whom he does not appear inclined to censure, or by that which he adopts for himself. Suppose the court had said: "Congress has judged of the necessity and propriety of this measure, and having exercised their undoubted functions in so deciding, it is not consistent with judicial modesty to say there is no such necessity, and thus to arrogate to ourselves the right of putting our *veto* upon a law."

Or suppose the court, after hearing a most elaborate and able argument on the constitutionality of the law, had said: "It is not our intention to bring that subject into discussion. We are willing to acquiesce in this particular case so long as the charter continues without being violated—because it has been repeatedly argued before Congress, and not only in 1791, but in 1815, was solemnly decided against the measure."

Would this reasoning have satisfied, or ought it to have satisfied the publick? Would Amphyction himself be content with the declaration of the Supreme Court that, on any question concerning the constitutionality of an act, it is enough to say "it is not consistent with judicial modesty" to contradict the opinion of Congress, and "thus to arrogate to themselves the right of putting their *veto* upon a law" or that "they are willing to acquiesce" in the particular act, "because it has been repeatedly argued before Congress, and not only in 1791, but in 1815," or at some other time since 1801, "was solemnly decided in favour of the measure?"

But if, as we must believe was the fact in this case, because it is so stated by the Judges, the court should be "unanimously and decidedly of opinion that the law is constitutional," would it comport with their honour, with their duty, or with truth, to insinuate an opinion that Congress had violated the constitution? If it would not, then was it incumbent on the court in this case, to pursue, not the course marked out by Amphyction but that which he censures. It was incumbent on them to state their real opinion and their reasons for it. Those reasons, I am persuaded, require only to be read with fairness and with attention to be approved.

April 28, 1819   A FRIEND TO THE UNION

Roane's "Hampden" Essays

Richmond Enquirer, June 11–22, 1819

As he had done for "Amphictyon" (see p. 52, above), Richmond Enquirer *editor Thomas Ritchie supplied an introductory paragraph for "Hampden"—his cousin Spencer Roane. At the head of the first "Hampden" essay, Ritchie wrote, under the admonition* HEAR HIM FOR HIS CAUSE:

"We ask the attention of our readers to the series of Numbers which will appear in succession under the venerable name of Hampden. *The subject is one which is* entitled *to the liveliest interest; and the pen of the writer is equal to the subject, great as it is, which he has undertaken to discuss. The Supreme Court of the United States is a tribunal of great and commanding authority; whose decisions, if not received as 'the law and the prophets,' are always entitled to the deepest attention. To the presiding Justice of that court, we are always ready to pay that tribute, which his great abilities deserve—but no tribunal, however high, no abilities, however splendid, ought to canonize the opinions which are advanced. We solemnly believe the opinion of the supreme court in the case of the bank to be fraught with alarming consequences, the federal constitution to be misinterpreted, and the rights of the states and the people to be threatened with danger. We solemnly believe, that Hampden has refuted the opinion of the supreme court, and placed it in its proper light before the public. We wish the people to hear him—'hear him for his cause.' "*

Roane supplied a heading for his essays that was repeated at the beginning of each one: "Rights of 'The States,' and of 'The People.' " To each printing of that title was anchored a footnote

consisting of the text of the Tenth Amendment, the most impor-
tant recognition of states' rights in the Constitution: "The powers
not delegated to the United States by the constitution, nor pro-
hibited by it to the states, are reserved to the states respectively,
or to the people."—GG.

I

And, for my part,
I know no personal cause to spurn at *them*,
But for the general: *they* would be crown'd.[1]

To the Editor of the Enquirer:

By means of a letter to you, sir, I beg leave to address my fellow citizens. I address them on a most momentous subject. I address them with diffidence, and with respect; with the respect
which is due to the most favored, if not the most respectable section of the human race: and with the diffidence which I ought to
feel, when I compare the smallness of my means, with the greatness of my undertaking. I address my fellow citizens without any
distinction of parties. Although some of them will, doubtless, lend
a more willing ear than others, to the important truths I shall endeavor to inculcate, none can hear them with indifference. None
of them can be prepared to give a Carte Blanche to our federal
rulers, and to obliterate the state governments, forever, from our
political system.

It has been the happiness of the American people to be connected together in a confederate republic: to be united by a system, which extends the sphere of popular government, and recon-
ciles the advantages of monarchy with those of a republic: a system, which combines all the internal advantages of the latter, with

[1] Marcus Brutus; in the tragedy of Julius Caesar—act 2d. [Roane substituted "them" and "they" for "him" and "he" respectively, and signaled
this change by the use of italics. —GG.]

all the force of the former.[2]—It has been our happiness to believe, that in the partition of powers between the general and state governments, the former possessed only such as were expressly granted, or passed therewith as necessary incidents, while all the residuary powers were retained by the latter. It was deemed by the enlightened founders of the constitution, as essential to the internal happiness and welfare of their constituents, to reserve some powers to the state governments; as to their external safety, to grant others to the government of the union. This, it is believed, was done by the constitution, in its original shape; but such were the natural fears and jealousies of our citizens, in relation to this all important subject, that it was deemed necessary to quiet those fears, by the 10th amendment to the constitution. It is not easy to devise stronger terms to effect that object, than those used in that amendment.

Such however is the proneness of all men to extend and abuse their power,—to "feel power and forget right,"—that even this article has afforded us no security. That legislative power which is every where extending the sphere of its activity and drawing all power into its impetuous vortex,[3] has blinked even the strong words of this amendment.—That judicial power, which, according to Montesquieu is, "in some measure, next to nothing;" and whose province this great writer limits, to "punishing criminals and determining the disputes which arise between individuals":—that judiciary which, in Rome, according to the same author, was not entrusted to decide questions which concerned "the interest of the state, in the relation which it bears to its citizens";[4] and which, in England, has only invaded the constitution in the worst of times, and then, always, on the side of arbitrary power, has also deemed its interference necessary, in our country.—It will readily be perceived that I allude to the decision of the supreme court of the

---

[2] Montesquieu, 1 vol. pa. 51. This form of government is eulogized in 1st Federalist, pa. 52.
[3] 2 vol. of Federalist, pa. 11, 19. Jefferson's Notes, pa. 215.
[4] Montesq. pa. 222, 226, 259.

United States, in the case of M'Culloh against the state of Maryland.

The warfare carried on by the legislature of the union against the rights of "the states" and of "the people" has been with various success[5] and always by detachment. *They* have not dared to break down the barriers of the constitution, by a *general* act declaratory of their power. That measure was too bold for these ephemeral deputies of the people.—That people hold them in check, by a short rein, and would consign them to merited infamy, at the next election. .... They have adopted a safer course. *Crescit Eundo* is their maxim; and they have succeeded in seeing the constitution expounded, not by what it actually contains, but by the *abuses* committed under it. A new mode of amending the constitution has been added to the ample ones provided in that instrument, and the strongest checks established in it, have been made to yield to the force of precedents! The time will soon arrive, if it is not already at hand, when the constitution may be expounded without ever looking into it!—by merely reading the acts of a renegado congress, or adopting the outrageous doctrines of Pickering, Lloyd, or Sheffey![6]

The warfare waged by the judicial body has been of a bolder

[5] Witness the memorable and unconstitutional alien and sedition laws, which were put down by the general rising of the people; and the second bank bill, which was lost by the casting vote of the venerable *Clinton*.

[6] In the debates on the bank bill of Jan. 1810, Mr. *Pickering* said—that in the affairs of a nation, whatever the public good requires to be done is *necessary* and *proper* to be done and that congress, in this respect, was like the state legislatures! Mr. Lloyd said—that if the country goes on increasing, as it has done, it is not improbable, but that the *defined* powers may prove only a *text*, and the *implied* powers furnish *the sermon* to it! Mr. Sheffey advocated the right of establishing banks as *instrumental* in giving effect to the delegated powers, and said, that congress may adopt *any measures*, which *they may deem* necessary and proper to accomplish the object, in *any manner*, whether these means be direct or *remote*! (See the speeches of these gentlemen.) Mr. Hamilton had before said: that it belongs to the *discretion* of the national legislature to "pronounce upon the objects which *concern* the *general welfare*," and to appropriate the money of the union to whatever *concerns* "the general interests of *learning*, of *agriculture*, of *manufactures*, and of *commerce*." (See his report of 5th Dec. 1791.)

tone and character. It was not enough for them to sanction, in former times, the detestable doctrines of Pickering & Co. as aforesaid: it was not enough for them to annihilate the freedom of the press, by incarcerating all those, who dared, with a manly freedom, to canvass the conduct of their public agents:[7] it was not enough for the predecessors of the present judges[8] to preach political sermons from the bench of justice, and bolster up the most unconstitutional measures, of the most abandoned of our rulers: it did not suffice to do the business in detail, and ratify, one by one, the legislative infractions of the constitution. That process would have been too slow, and perhaps too troublesome. It was possible, also, that some *Hampden* might make a stand, against some ship-money measure of the government, and although he would lose his cause with the court, might ultimately gain it with the *people*. They resolved, therefore, to put down all discussions of the kind, in future, by a judicial *coup de main*: to give a *general* letter of attorney to the future legislators of the union: and to tread under foot all those parts and articles of the constitution which had been, heretofore, deemed to set limits to the power of the federal legislature. That man must be a deplorable idiot who does not see that there is no earthly difference between an *unlimited* grant of power, and a grant limited in its terms, but accompanied with *unlimited* means of carrying it into execution.[9]

The supreme court of the United States have not only granted this *general* power of attorney to congress, but they have gone out of the record to do it, in the case in question. It was only necessary, in that case, to decide whether or not the bank law was "necessary and proper," within the meaning of the constitution, for carrying into effect some of the granted powers; but the court have, in effect, expunged those words from the constitution.

---

[7] In the cases of Lyon, Cooper and others.

[8] I mention it to the *honor* of the present judges, that they have given up the practice.

[9] In Madison's report, pa. 77, this idea is explicitly stated.

There is no essential difference between expunging words from an instrument, by erasure, and reading them in a sense entirely arbitrary with the reader, and which they do not naturally bear.[10] Great as is the confidence of the nation in all its tribunals, they are not at liberty to change the meaning of our language. I might therefore justly contend, that this opinion of the court, in so far as it outgoes the actual case depending before it, and so far as it established a *general* and *abstract* doctrine, was entirely extrajudicial, and without authority.—I shall not, however, press this point, as it is entirely merged in another, which I believe will be found conclusive;—namely, that that court had no power to adjudicate away the *reserved* rights of a sovereign member of the confederacy, and vest them in the general government.

It results from these remarks, Mr. Editor, that my opinion is, that the supreme court had no jurisdiction justifying the judgment which it gave, & that it decided the question wrongly. The power of the supreme court is indeed great, but it does not extend to every thing; it is not great enough to *change* the constitution. . . . These points I shall endeavor to maintain, in one or more subsequent numbers. I shall also briefly touch upon the bank law of the United States. That law is neither justified by the constitution, nor ratified by any acquiescence.

Had this opinion of the supreme court, however, not been pronounced, I should not have deemed it necessary to address the public, on the subject. I should not have been moved by any *particular* measure of aggression. I know full well, that however guarded our constitution may be, we must submit to particular infractions of it.—I know that our forefathers, of glorious and revolutionary memory, submitted to many *particular* acts of oppression, inflicted upon them by the British parliament. I know that "all experience hath shewn that mankind are more disposed

[10] Vattel tells us, pa. 374, that in the interpretation of treaties, *pacts* and promises, we ought not to deviate from *the common use of language,* unless there be strong reasons for it.

to suffer while evils are sufferable, than to right themselves by abolishing the forms to which they are accustomed:"[11]—and I know that it was only the *general* declaration by the British parliament, of their right "to legislate for us in all cases whatsoever,"[12] that combined the American people, as one man, against the oppressions of the British tyrant.

Such a declaration is now at hand. It exists, in the opinion of the supreme court. If the limits imposed on the general government, by the constitution, are stricken off, they have, *literally*, the power to legislate for us "in all cases whatsoever:" and then we may bid a last adieu to the state governments.

In discussing these momentous questions, I shall not hesitate to speak with the spirit of a freeman. I shall not be over-awed by the parasites of a government gigantic in itself, and inflated with recent victories. I love the honor, and, if you please the glory of my country, but I love its liberty better. Truth and liberty are dearer to me than Plato or Socrates.—I speak only of the measures of our public functionaries, but of them I shall speak freely. I am not a political surgeon: but this I know, that a wound which threatens to be mortal, must be probed to the bottom. The crisis is one which portends destruction to the liberties of the American people.

I address you, Mr. Editor, on this great subject with no sanguine presages of success. I must say to my fellow citizens, that they are sunk in apathy, and that a torpor has fallen upon them. Instead of that noble and magnanimous spirit which achieved our independence, and has often preserved us since, we are sodden in the *luxuries* of banking.[13] A money-loving, funding, stock-jobbing spirit has taken foothold among us. We are almost prepared to sell our liberties for "a mess of pottage."[14]—If Mason or Henry could lift their patriot heads from the grave, while they mourned

---

[11] Declaration of independence.   [12] Const. of Virginia, preamble.
[13] I fear many of our citizens will think I am *ironical.*
[14] Genesis, ch. 25, v. 34.

the complete fulfilment of their prophecies! they would almost exclaim with Jugurtha, "Venal people! you will soon perish, if you can find a purchaser."[15]

In examining this great subject, I shall only resort to authorities the most unquestionable. I shall *chiefly* test my doctrines, by those of the enlightened *advocates* of the constitution, at the time of its adoption. I shall also resort to a book, written, at least in part, by one of the highest-toned statesmen in America. That book is "The Federalist," and the writer alluded to, is Mr. Hamilton. The authors of that book have been eulogised by the Chief Justice, in his life of Washington, for their talents and love of union; and by the Supreme Court, in the opinion before us. The court has even gone so far as to say, that as to the opinions contained in that book, "no tribute can be paid to their *worth*, which exceeds their *merit*."—If I have any adversaries in this discussion, these *advocates* and this book are *their* witnesses, and I shall take leave to cross-examine them. That witness is the best for the defendant, who is produced on the part of the plaintiff: and he is most to be believed, who is both lauded by the court, and testifies against his interest or his prejudices.—I shall also use, occasionally, the celebrated report to the legislature of Virginia, in the year 1799. It has often been called by an eloquent statesman,[16]— his political bible. For truth, perspicuity and moderation, it has never been surpassed. It is entirely federal.[17]—It was the *Magna Charta* on which the republicans settled down, after the great struggle in the year 1799. Its principles have only *been departed* from since,[18]—by turn-coats and apostates. The principles of this report equally consult the rights and happiness of the several states, and the safety and independence of the union.

I shall commence, in the next number, *some* examination of the

[15] "Venalis civitas mox peritura, si emptorem invenias."
[16] Mr. John Randolph.
[17] I use this term here in its *true* sense, and as opposed to consolidation.
[18] This remark applies, of course, only to republicans.

opinion of the Supreme Court. It is in every respect entitled to the chief notice. I have great reason to distrust myself in this undertaking. I am provided with a sling and a stone, but I fear the inspiration will be wanting.[19]—I consider that opinion as the "*Alpha* and *Omega*, the beginning and the *end*, the first and the *last*[20]—of federal usurpations."

June 11, 1819   HAMPDEN

II

> The grievances by which we are oppressed, I draw
> under two heads: acts of power against law, and the
> judgments of lawyers against our liberty.[1]

To the Editor of the Enquirer:

According to the regular course of legal proceedings I ought, in the first place, to urge my plea in abatement to the jurisdiction of the court. As, however, we are not now in a court of justice, and such a course might imply some want of confidence in the merits of my cause, I will postpone that enquiry, for the present, and proceed directly to the merits. In investigating those merits, I shall sometimes discuss particular points stated by the supreme court, and, at others, urge propositions inconsistent with them. I pledge myself to object to nothing in the opinion in question, which does not appear to me to be materially subject to error.

I beg leave to lay down the following propositions, as being equally incontestable in themselves, and assented to by the enlightened *advocates* of the constitution, at the time of its adoption.

1. That that constitution conveyed only a limited grant of powers to the general government, and reserved the residuary powers to the governments of the states, and to the people: and that the 10th amendment was merely declaratory of this principle, and

---

[19] 1 Samuel—ch. 36, v. 45.   [20] Revelations, ch. 22, v. 13.

[1] Speech of Sir Ro: Philips. 6 Hume, 179.

inserted only to quiet what the court is pleased to call, "the excessive jealousies of the people."[2]

2. That the limited grant to congress of certain enumerated powers, only carried with it such additional powers as were *fairly incidental* to them, or, in other words, were necessary and proper for their execution.

And 3dly, that the insertion of the words "necessary and proper," in the last part of the 8th section of the 1st article, did not enlarge the powers previously given, but were inserted only through abundant caution.

On the first point it is to be remarked that the constitution does not give to congress *general* legislative powers, but the legislative powers *"herein granted."* . . . 1st art. of Const. . . . . So it is said in "The Federalist,"[3] that the jurisdiction of the general government extends to certain enumerated objects only, and leaves to the states a residuary and inviolable sovereignty over all other objects; that in the *new* as well as the old government, the general powers are limited, and the states, in all the unenumerated cases, are left in the enjoyment of their sovereign and independent jurisdiction:[4] that the powers given to the general government are few and defined:[5] and that all authorities of which the states are not *explicitly* divested, in favor of the union, remain with them in full force; as is admitted by the affirmative grants to the general government, and the prohibitions of some powers, by negative clauses, to the state governments.[6]

It was said by Mr. Madison, in the convention of Virginia, that the powers of the general government were enumerated, and that its legislative powers are on defined objects, beyond which it cannot extend its jurisdiction[7]: that the general government has no power but what is given and delegated, and that the delegation

---

[2] The present discussion shows that those jealousies were not without foundation.

[3] 1 Federalist, pa. 259. [4] Ib. pa. 265.
[5] Ib. pa. 308. [6] Ib. pa. 205.
[7] Debates Convention Virginia, pa. 76.

alone warranted the power:[8] and that the powers of the general government are but *few*, and relate to external objects, whereas those of the states relate to those great objects which immediately concern the prosperity of the people.[9] It was said by Mr. Marshall, that congress cannot go beyond the delegated powers, and that a law not warranted by any of the enumerated powers would be void:[10] and that the powers not given to congress, were *retained* by the states, and THAT without the aid of implication.[11] Mr. Randolph said, that every power not given by this system is left with the states.[12] And it was said by Mr. Geo. Nicholas, that the people retain the powers not conferred on the general government, and that congress cannot meddle with a power not enumerated.[13]

It was resolved by the legislature of Virginia, in acting upon the celebrated report of 1799 (of which Mr. Madison, the great patron of the constitution, was the author), that the powers vested in the general government result from the *compact*, to which the *states* are parties; that they are limited by the plain sense of that instrument (the constitution), and extend no further than they are authorised by the grant:[14] that the constitution had been constantly discussed and justified, by *its friends*, on the ground that the powers not given to the government were withheld from it: and that if any doubts could have existed on the original text of the constitution, they are removed by the 10th amendment:[15] that if the powers granted be valid, it is only because they are *granted*, and that all others are retained:[16] that both from the original constitution and the 10th amendment, it results that it is incumbent on the general government to *prove*, from the constitution, that it grants the *particular* power:[17] that it is *immaterial* whether unlimited powers be exercised under the name of un-

[8] Ib. pa. 417.
[9] Ib. pa. 188.
[10] Ib. 393.
[11] Ib. 298.
[12] Ib. 151.
[13] Ib. 179.
[14] In Madison's Report, 35.
[15] Ib. 36.
[16] Madison's Report, 37.
[17] Ib. 19.

limited powers, or under that of unlimited means of carrying a limited power into execution:[18] that in all the discussions and ratifications of the constitution, it was urged as a characteristic of the government, that powers not given were retained, and that none were given but those which were *expressly* granted, or were FAIRLY INCIDENT[19] to them: and that in the ratification of the constitution by Virginia, it was expressly asserted, that every power *not granted* by the constitution, remained with them (the people of Virginia), and *at their will.*[20]

2. I am to shew in the second place that by the provisions of the constitution (taken in exclusion of the words "necessary and proper" in the 8th § of the 1st article) such powers were only conveyed, to the general government, as were expressly granted, or were (to use the language of the report) FAIRLY INCIDENT to them. I shall afterwards shew, that the insertion of those words, in that article, made no difference whatever, and created no extension of the powers previously granted.

I take it to be a clear principle of universal law—of the law of nature, of nations, of war, of reason, and of the common law— that the general grant of a thing or power, carries with it all those means (and those only) which are necessary to the perfection of the grant, or the execution of the power. All those codes entirely *concur* in this respect, and are bottomed upon a clear principle. That principle is one, which, while it completely effects the object of the grant or power, is a safe one, as it relates to the reserved rights of the other party. This is the true principle, and it is an universal one applying to *all* pacts and conventions, high or low, or of what nature or kind soever. It cannot be stretched or extended, even in relation to the American government; although, for purposes which can easily be conjectured, the supreme court has used high sounding words as to it. They have stated it to be a

[18] Ib. 77.　　　　　　　　　[19] Ib. 83.
[20] Ib. 93.

government extending from St. Croix to the Gulf of Mexico, and from the Atlantic to the Pacific Ocean. This principle depends on a basis which applies to all cases whatsoever, and is inflexible and universal.

If, in relation to the powers of the general government, the express grants, aided by this principle under its true limitation, do not confer on that government powers sufficiently ample, let those powers be extended by an amendment to the constitution. Let us now do what our convention did in 1787, in relation to the articles of confederation. Let us extend their powers, but let this be the act of the *people*, and not that of subordinate agents. But let us see how far the amendments *are* to extend, and not, by opening wide the door of implied or constructive powers, grant we know not how much, nor enter into a field of indeterminable limits. Let us, in the language of the venerable *Clinton*,[21] extend the powers of the general government, if it be necessary; but until they are extended, let us only exercise such powers as are clear and undoubted.

In making some quotations from the laws of nature, of nations, of war, of reason, and the common law, it will be seen that these establish not only the principle I contend for, but the *limits* under which the incidental powers are to be exercised. It is in this last relation that I ask the principal attention of the reader. While these limits must always, in a degree, depend upon the circumstances of every particular case, the cases I shall quote give the general character of the power. It will be seen that that power is always limited by necessity; which, although it may not be, in all cases, a sheer necessity, falls far short of the extensive range claimed, in this instance, by the supreme court. I need not say to the legal part of our citizens, that the exception proves the rule: nor that the allowance of a power *up to* a given limit, is a denial of it beyond it.

We are told by Vattel that "since a nation is obliged to preserve

---

[21] In his rejection, as vice president, of the second bank bill.

itself, it has a right to every thing *necessary* for its preservation, for that the *law of nature* gives us a right to every thing WITHOUT WHICH we could not fulfil an obligation: otherwise it would oblige us to do *impossibilities*, or rather contradict itself, in prescribing a duty and prohibiting, at the same time, the *only means* of fulfilling it."[22] Again he tells us, that a nation has a right to every thing *without which* it cannot obtain the perfection of the members, and the state.[23] Again we are told, by him, that a tacit faith may be given by a prince, &c. and that "every thing *without which* what is agreed upon, cannot take place," is tacitly granted—as, if a promise is made to an army of the enemy, which has advanced far into the country "that it shall return home in safety," *provisions* are also granted, for they cannot return *without them.* . . . We are further told that in granting or accepting an interview *full security* is also tacitly granted.[24] The *provisions* and the *security* are each of them a *sine qua non* of the fulfilment of the grant, or promise: they are both *indispensible.*—So he tells us, that if a man grants to one his house, and to another his garden, the *only* entrance into which is through the house, the right of going through the house passes as an incident, for that it is absurd to give a garden to a man, into which he could not enter.[25] We are further told by this writer, that the grant of a passage for troops includes every thing connected with the passage, and *without which* it would not be practicable, as exercising military discipline, buying provisions, &c.:[26] that he who promises *security* to another by a safe conduct, is not only to forbear violating it himself, but also to *punish* those who do and compel them to make reparation:[27] that a safe conduct naturally includes the baggage of the party, and every thing *necessary* for the journey, but that the *safest* and *modern* way is, to *particularize* even the baggage:[28] and that a permission to *settle* any where, includes the wife and children, for

[22] Vattel, pa. 22.
[24] Ib. 334, 354.
[26] Ib. 514.
[28] Ib. 617.

[23] Ib. pa. 23.
[25] Ib. 390.
[27] Ib. 615.

that when a man settles any where he carries his wife and children with him—but that the case is different as to a safe conduct, for that when a man travels, his family is usually left at home.[29]

These examples quoted from the laws of nature, of nations, and of war, have a remarkable and entire coincidence with the principles of the common law, and shew that great principles extend themselves alike, into every code. In all of them the incidental power is limited to what is *necessary*: and in none of them is a latitude allowed, as extensive as that claimed by the supreme court.

The principle of the common law, is, that when any one grants a thing he grants also that *without which* the grant cannot have its effect;[30] as, if I grant you my trees in a wood, you may come with carts over my land to carry the wood off. So a right of way arises on the same principle of *necessity*, by operation of law; as, if a man grants me a piece of land in the middle of his field, he tacitly and impliedly gives me a right to come at it.[31] We are again told, that when the law giveth any thing to any one, it impliedly giveth whatever is necessary for taking or enjoying the same: it giveth "what is *convenient*, viz. entry, egress and regress as much as is *necessary*."[32] The term "convenient" is here used in a sense convertible with the term "necessary," and is not allowed the latitude of meaning given to it by the supreme court. It is so restricted in tenderness to the rights of the other party. The right of way, passing in the case above mentioned, is also that, merely, of a *private* way, and does not give a high road, or avenue, through another's land, though such might be most *convenient* to the purposes of the grantee. It is also a principle of the common law that the incident is to be taken according to "a *reasonable* and *easy*

---

[29] Ib. 617.
[30] II Report, 52, Kuivet's case—"Lex est cuicunque aliquis quid concedit, concedere videtur et id *sine quo* res ipsa esse non potuit."
[31] 2 Bl. Comm. 36.
[32] Co. Litt. 56a.

sense," and not strained to comprehend things remote, "unlikely or unusual."[33] The connexion between the grant and the incident must be easy and clear: the grant does not carry with it as incidents, things which are remote or doubtful.

These quotations from the common law are conclusive in favor of a restricted construction of the incidental powers.—They shew that nothing is granted but what is *necessary*. They exclude every thing that is only *remotely* necessary, or which only *tends* to the fulfilment.

These doctrines of the common law control the present case. But it is immaterial, as I have already said, by what code it is to be tested. On this point, there is no difference between them; for they all depend upon an inflexible and immutable principle. The common law, however, governs this case. That law is often resorted to, of necessity, in expounding the constitution. . . . Many of the powers given by the constitution, are given in terms only known in the common law. The authority of that law is universally admitted to a certain extent in expounding the constitution.— It is admitted both by the report of 1799, and by the Virginia legislature of the same year, in relation to such parts thereof as have a sanction from the constitution by the technical phrases used therein, expressing the powers given to the general government, and also as to such parts thereof as may be adopted by Congress, as necessary and proper for carrying into execution the powers expressly delegated.[34] Is not this admission full up to the very point of referring to that law in this case, and adopting the standard which it has established?

That law not only affords this standard, but it was wise in the constitution to refer to a standard which is equally familiar to all the states, and is corroborated by the corresponding principles of every other code. By the common law, the term *incident* is also

[33] 3 Bac. Abridg. 395.
[34] Madison's Report, pa. 67; and instructions of Jan. 11, 1800 to the senators of Virginia.

well defined, as the examples I have quoted will shew.—It is the part of wisdom to define the terms as you go, or at least to refer to a standard which contains their definition. I have another preference for this code, and for the term "incident" which it uses, and that is that that term is *particular*. The term "means," started up on the present occasion, is not only undefined, but is *general*: and *"dolus latet in generalibus."* . . .[35] Why should the supreme court trump up a term on this occasion, which is equally novel, undefined, and *general?* Why should they select a term which is broad enough to demolish the limits prescribed to the general government, by the constitution?—I will now proceed to shew that the terms "necessary" and *"incidental* powers," were those uniformly used at the outset of the constitution—while the term "means" is entirely of modern origin. It is at least so, when offered as a substitute for the terms "incident," or "incidental powers."

We are told in the Federalist[36] that all "powers *indispensably necessary,* are granted by the constitution, though they be not expressly granted"; and that all the particular powers *requisite* to carry the enumerated ones into effect, would have resulted to the government by unavoidable implication, *without* the words "necessary and proper"; and that when a power is given, every particular power *necessary* for doing it is included. Again[37] it is said that a power is nothing but the ability or faculty of doing a thing, and that that ability includes the means *necessary* for its execution.

It is laid down in the *report* before mentioned, that congress under the terms "necessary and proper," have only all *incidental* powers necessary and proper, &c. and that the only enquiry is whether the power is properly an *incident* to an express power and *necessary* to its execution, and that if it is not, congress cannot ex-

[35] Guile covers itself under general expressions.
[36] 1 vol. pa. 256.   [37] Ib. 205.

ercise it: and that this construction prevailed during all the discussions and ratifications of the constitution, and is *absolutely necessary* to *consist* with the idea of defined or particular powers: Again it is said, that none but the express powers and those *fairly incident* to them were granted by the constitution.[38]

The terms "incident" and "incidental powers" are not only the terms used in the early stages, and by the *friends* of the constitution, but they are the terms used by the *court* itself, in more passages than one, in relation to the power in question. The same terms are used by the Chief Justice in his Life of Washington (5 vol. 293) as relative to the implied powers. So it is said by Mr. *Clinton*, in his rejection of the bank bill before mentioned, that the means must be *accessorial* and *subordinate* to the end. Mr. *Clay*[39] also said on the same occasion that the implied powers must be *accessorial* and *obviously flow* from the enumerated ones.— Having shewn this universal adoption of these terms, we will now recur to their real meaning. In *Co. Litt.* 151 b. an incident is defined, in the common law, to be a thing "*appertaining* to or *following* another as more worthy or *principal*." So Johnson defines it to be "means falling in beside the *main* design." Can it be then said, that means which are of an independent or *paramount* character can be implied as incidental ones? Certainly not, unless, to say the least, they be absolutely necessary.

Can it be said after this that we are at liberty to invent terms, at our pleasure, in relation to this all important question? Are we not tied down to the terms used by the founders of the constitution; terms too, of limited, well defined, and established signification? On the contrary, I see great danger in using the *general* term now introduced: It may cover the latent designs of

---

[38] Madison's Report, pa. 75, 76, 83.
[39] I quote Mr. Clay not more from his high standing in the government, than for the *liberality* with which he is known to expound the powers of the general government.

ambition, and change the nature of the general government. It is entirely unimportant, as is before said, by what means this end is effected.

3. I come in the third place to shew that the words "necessary and proper," in the constitution, add nothing to the powers before given to the general government. They were only added (says the Federalist)[40] for greater caution, and are tautologous and redundant, though *harmless*.—It is also said in the *report* aforesaid[41] that these words *do not amount* to a grant of *new* power, but for the removal of all uncertainty, the declaration was made that the means were included in the grant. I might multiply authorities on this point to infinity; but if these no not suffice, neither would one were he to arise from the dead. If this power existed in the government, before these words were used, its repetition or reduplication, in the constitution, does not increase it. The "expression of that which before existed in the grant, has no operation." . . .[42] So these words "necessary and proper" have no greater or other effect than if they had been annexed to, and repeated in, every specific grant;[43] and in that case they would have been equally unnecessary and harmless. As a friend, however, to the just powers of the general government, I do not object to them, considered as merely declaratory words, and inserted for greater caution: I only deny to them an extension to which they are not entitled, and which may be fatal to the reserved rights of the states and of the people.

In my next number, Mr. Editor, I shall examine, more particularly, SOME of the principles contained in the opinion of the supreme court.

June 15, 1819   HAMPDEN

---

[40] 1 Fed. pa. 207.
[41] Madison's Report, pa. 75.
[42] "Expressio eorum quæ tacite insunt, nihil operatur."
[43] 1 Fed. pa. 206.

III

Let us not act like Cambyses's Judges, who when their approbation was demanded by the prince, to some illegal measure, said, that, *though there was a written law, the Persian Kings might follow their own will and pleasure.*[1]

To the Editor of the Enquirer:

I trust I have shewn, by the preceding detail, that the words "necessary and proper," contained in the constitution, were tautologous and redundant, and carried nothing more to the general government than was conveyed by the general grant of a specified power. I have also shewn, that, in that case, such means were implied, and such only, as were *essential* to effectuate the power: and that this is the case, in all the codes, of the law of nature, of nations, of war, of reason, and the common law. The means, and the only means, admitted by them all, and especially by the common law, are laid down, emphatically, to be such, *without which* the grant cannot have its effect: and I have also endeavored to shew that by that law, the construction in this case is to be governed. In all these codes this implied and ulterior power has the same limitation. In none of them is a claim as extensive as that asserted by the supreme court, recognized or tolerated; while, on the other hand, claims far inferior in point of latitude have been often reprobated. This principle, while it carries to the grantee what is necessary, carries nothing more. It respects the rights of both the parties. It remembers that there is a grantor, as well as a grantee. It recognizes the golden principle *"sic utere tuo ut alienum non ladis."* But when you get beyond this criterion of necessity, you embark in a field without limits; and every thing then depending on *discretion*, the rights of the weaker party will be swept away. This principle, so sacred in all the codes, exists, emphatically, in

[1] Speech of Sir Francis Seymour. 6 Hume, 177.

ours, in which the constitution has imposed *express* limits to the granted powers by the strong words used in the 10th amendment. The supreme court has said that there is no expression in the constitution, like those in the former confederation, excluding implied or incidental powers. While this is admitted, it is denied that any greater latitude is given to these powers by the constitution, than they possess under the law of reason and justice, under the great principle which runs through all the codes. If there be any clause in the constitution having that effect, let it be pointed out. There is none such, and it is incumbent on the party claiming an extension of the general principle, to shew that such extension has been made. The state governments being originally in possession of all the legislative powers, are still to retain such as are not *shewn* to have been relinquished.

The supreme court, sensible of this necessity, and not being able to shew a specific extension of the principle, have argued in favor of an enlarged construction, by saying that these terms "necessary and proper," are placed in the constitution among the *powers*, and not among the limitations on those powers. If the object in using them was merely for greater caution, and to put down all uncertainty on the subject, *that* was the proper place for them. It would have been wrong to have placed them among the prohibitions, as they are not pretended to *prohibit* any thing to the general government: it is only contended that they create no enlargement of the powers previously given. In what place, therefore, could these words have been so properly inserted?

The court is also pleased to say, that these terms *purport* to enlarge the powers previously given. It is difficult to see how a reiteration of the words can increase the power; and it is unimportant whether that power was merely implied or was expressed. A given power is not enlarged by being merely repeated. The supreme court itself admits that these terms were used, and *only used* to remove all doubts of the implied powers of the national legislature, in relation to the great mass of concerns entrusted to it.—This is an admission by the court that they were not used for the purpose of *enlargement*; and it is entirely inconsistent with their other pretension, that these words were put in, or purported, to enlarge the powers.

The supreme court has also claimed such enlargement on the ground, that our constitution is one of a vast republic, whose limits they have pompously swelled, and greatly exaggerated. The high sounding words they have used, in describing those limits, cannot alter the force of great principles. The constitution is a *compact* between the people of each state, and those of all the states, and it is nothing more than a compact. The principles I have mentioned are immutable, and apply to *all* compacts. It is entirely unimportant, whether the territory to which the compact relates, extends from "Indus to the pole," or be no larger than that of the county of Warwick. There is no code which graduates this principle, by the extent of the territory to which it relates.

The supreme court has also claimed favour, in this particular, on the ground of the magnitude of the trust confided to the general government. If that trust be great, neither is that reserved to the state governments small, or unimportant. On this point, let what the court is pleased to call, "the excessive jealousies" of the states, stand as an authority. That trust is not small or unimportant, which produced these jealousies: jealousies which could only be quieted by the strong words of reservation, contained in the 10th amendment to the constitution.—That trust is not small, which relates to "those great objects which immediately concern the prosperity of the people."[2]

The court is pleased to remind us, with the same view, that it is a *constitution* we are expounding. That constitution, however, conveys only *limited* and specified powers to the government, the extent of which must be traced in the instrument itself. The residuary powers abide in the state governments, and the people.

[2] Mr. Madison. Debates Vir. Con. pa. 188.

If it is a constitution, it is also a *compact* and a limited and de-fined compact. The states have also constitutions, and their people rights, which ought also to be respected. It is in behalf of these constitutions, and these rights, that the enlarged and boundless power of the general government is objected to. . . . The construc-tion which gives it, is in entire derogation of them.

It is said by the supreme court, that a constitution cannot se-lect among the various means which may be found necessary, in the execution of the granted powers. This is distinctly admitted: but the constitution ought to establish, as ours has established, a *criterion* in relation to them: and that criterion should be the *law* to the several departments, in making *their* selection. That cri-terion is afforded in the present instance, by the means being "nec-essary and proper," to the execution of the power, or not so, as the case may be. . . . A choice may safely be left to congress, *within* that limit: but if their choice of means is to go beyond it, and to range at large, without stint or limits, it is in vain to talk of its being a limited government. That government is one of unlim-ited powers, which is at liberty to use means which are *unlimited*.

The supreme court has said that congress must "according to the *dictates of reason* be permitted to select the means." What then becomes of the terms "necessary and proper?" They further say that those who object to their using any *appropriate* means must shew that it is *excepted*. On the contrary we are told by the *report*, and by all the authorities, that "it is incumbent on the gen-eral government to *prove* that the constitution grants the *par-ticular* power."

The supreme court seems to consider it as quite unimportant, so long as the great principles involving human liberty are not invaded, by which set of the representatives of the people, the powers of government are to be exercised. I beg leave to say, on the other hand, that the adjustment of those powers made by the constitution, between the general and state governments, is beyond their power, and ought not to be set aside. That adjustment has been made by the *people* themselves, and they only are competent to change it. It ought to be respected by the functionaries of both governments.—The rights of the states ought not to be usurped and taken from them; for the powers delegated to the general government are few and defined, and relate chiefly to external objects,[3] while the states retain a residuary and inviolable sovereignty over all other subjects;[4] over all those great subjects which immediately concern the prosperity of the people.[5] Are these last powers of so trivial a character that it is entirely unimportant which of the governments acts upon them? Are the representatives of Connecticut in congress, best qualified to make laws, on the subject of our negro population? or ought the South Carolina nabobs to regulate *their* steady habits?—Is it the wish of any state, or at least of any of the larger states, that the whole circle of legislative powers should be confided to a body in which, in one branch at least, the small state of Delaware has as much weight as the great state of New York; having fourteen times its population? The supreme court thinks such a change as this entirely unimportant. On this, as on other occasions, I would "render unto Cæsar the things which are Cæsar's." I would construe the constitution as it really is.

The supreme court is of opinion, that a government having such ample powers as that of the union, should have ample means for their execution. Within the criterion I have contended for, this is admitted: beyond that criterion, the position is denied. If this criterion be inadequate to the true interests of the union, let the supreme court shew it to the *people*, or to the next convention, and these means will be enlarged. They will, in that case, be enlarged by the only competent power. With the supreme court the question, and the only question, was, what powers and what means

[3] 1 Fed. 398.   [4] Ib. 259.
[5] Debates Vir. Con. pa. 188.

have been granted. The *powers* of the old confederation were sufficiently ample. They extended at least to making war and peace, which so vitally involve human happiness: but the *means* of carrying on a war, it did not possess. For those means, congress were entirely dependent on the state governments. The means were not stretched up, by construction, to equal the acknowledged amplitude of the powers. No court or congress dared to do this: but an appeal was made to the people, in convention, and they amplified the means, by the present constitution. This is a case exactly in point, and determines the course proper to be pursued, if indeed the true principle relative to implied powers is not sufficiently extensive.

Indeed, Mr. Editor, the great fault of the present times is, in considering the constitution as perfect. It is considered as a nose of wax, and is stretched and contradicted at the arbitrary will and pleasure of those who are entrusted to administer it. It is considered as *perfect*, in contravention of the opinion of those who formed it. Their opinion is greatly manifested, in the ample provisions it contains for its amendment. It is so considered in contravention of every thing that is human: for nothing made by man is perfect. It is construed to this effect, by the *in's*, to the prejudice of the *out's*; by the agents of one government in prejudice of the rights of another; and by those who, possessing power, will not fail to "feel it, and forget right."

The supreme court has said, that it is a clear proposition, that the general government, though limited in its powers, is supreme within the sphere of its action: and again, that the government, though limited in its powers, is supreme. The court had before admitted, in terms, that the government could only exercise the powers granted to it. I do not understand this jargon. This word "supreme" does not sound well in a government which acts under a limited constitution. The *people* only are supreme. The constitution is subordinate to them, and the departments of the government are subordinate to that constitution. To use the language of

the report of 1799,[6] "the authority of constitutions over governments, and of the people over constitutions, are truths which
should be ever kept in mind." If the court only means that the
government is supreme *up to* the limits of the constitution, and
no further, there is no difference of opinion between us; but, in
that case, their language is inaccurate. A body which is subordinate to a compact, which is subordinate to another body, can
scarcely be said to be supreme.

The supreme court have said, that the great powers granted to
the government cannot be supposed to draw after them, such
powers only, as are *inferior*. I have already given an answer to this
position: in addition, I will say that the powers taken into the
service must be "necessary and proper."—It is a sophism to say,
that the annexation of the last word to the first enlarges *its* signification: both these terms are requisite to define, completely, the
character of the power. It must be one which is not only proper,
that is peculiar to that end, but also necessary. I shall refer more
particularly, presently, to the meaning of these terms.

The court is of opinion that the right to establish a bank stands
on the same foundation with that to exact oaths of office, and that
he would be charged with insanity who would deny to congress
the latter power. Of banks I shall presently shew, that while they
are not necessary to the execution of any power, they cut deeply
into the reserved rights of the several states. In both these respects
the case of oaths is widely different. . . . I would charge *him* with
insanity who would say that under the actual state of the world
they are not necessary. They impose on *some* men, at least, a solemn obligation to tell the truth: they do it by appealing to a future state of rewards and punishments. The convention itself has
settled this point by exacting an oath from the *president* and from
other public agents. If it is necessary for the highest officer in the
government to stand under this solemn sanction, much more

---

[6] Report of 1799, pa. 41.

ought those who are inferior.—So while these oaths are necessary, they are entirely *harmless*. . . . They invade no rights of the state governments, or of the people: and the ground on which the objection rests in the case before us, has no existence as to them.

The denial of the right to establish banks is also said, by the supreme court, to carry with it the denial of that of annexing punishments to crimes. . . . That punishment is indispensably necessary: it is a *sine qua non* of the prohibition of crimes. A penal law without a sanction is unknown among civilized men; and that sanction is always *vindicatory* rather than remuneratory.[7]

Several other cases put by the supreme court on this head stand on the same foundation and are susceptible of the same answer. In all the other cases, also, the powers implied are *necessary* to effect the specific objects of the grant. So, on the other hand, they work no injury to the rights of the states or of the people.

What are we to think of the case before us, when the analogies resorted to, to support it, are so widely different from it?

The supreme court is further of opinion, that the power of incorporating banks is justified by the admitted right of congress to establish governments, for the vacant territories of the United States; which governments are also said to be corporations.—It is astonishing that the court did not perceive the difference. Those territories have no other local legislatures, but the congress: and consequently, congress has the same power in them, in this particular, as the state governments have, in the several states. The erection of such governments also invades no right of any state: it is not only *harmless* as to the states, but absolutely necessary for the preservation of this part of the public property. This power is as harmless as to the states, as that, even, of imposing oaths.—This view of the subject makes it unnecessary to consider the effect of another provision in the constitution—authorizing congress to

---

[7] 1 Bl. Com. pa. 56.

make "all needful rules and regulations" in regard to such territories. These words, alone, it is at present supposed, would be sufficient to carry the power.

I come now, to ascertain, more particularly, the meaning of the terms "necessary and proper," used in the constitution. I have, before me, Johnson's Dictionary, which is believed to be the best in the English language. By it I find that "necessary" means "needful," "indispensably requisite:" and that "proper" means "peculiar," "not common or belonging to more."—To justify a measure under the constitution it must, therefore, be either "necessary and proper," or which is the same thing "indispensably requisite" and "peculiar" to the execution of a given power. So far from the bank of the United States being *peculiar* to any of the given powers, its friends have not yet agreed upon the particular power to which it is to be attached! Hence it is, that the present bank law is wholly *without* a preamble, stating the grounds on which it was predicated. At the same time that congress were under this inability, they were not able to agree with Mr. Hamilton, as to the grounds of the first bank law, nor with the supreme court. They could not agree with Mr. Hamilton, that it should be adopted because it would be "*conducive* to the successful conducting of the national finances, *tend* to *give facility* to the obtaining of loans and be *productive* of considerable advantage to trade and industry in general." The supreme court has admitted an incorporation not to be *peculiar* to any of the powers, by contending that it is a means common to many ends, such as building cities and the like. This power, therefore, to say the least, is not *peculiar* or *necessary* to the execution of any of the granted powers; and Mr. Hamilton has himself admitted this, by using the diffuse and ductile terms contained in the preamble to his bill. I will ask with Madison, in his celebrated speech against the first bank law, is it possible to consider these words used by Mr. Hamilton, as synonymous with the words "necessary and proper," used in the constitution?

Having shewn what the true meaning of these words is, I repeat that it is an universal rule of construction in relation to all treaties, *pacts* and promises, that we ought not to deviate from the common use of language unless we have the strongest reasons for it.[8]— These reasons are in this case, the other way. Again we are told that where a *pact* or treaty is expressed in clear terms, there is no reason to refuse them the sense they naturally bear.[9] Unless you take the words before us in their natural and proper sense, every thing belonging to the states will be swept away. They will be ingulfed in the vortex of the general government.

Yet the supreme court has said, that the term "necessary" frequently means "convenient or useful," and that it sometimes means *"conducive to."* This last sense of the word is at least not its natural sense, and has not been revived before, since the days of Mr. Hamilton, and of the famous sedition law. It opens too wide a door, to the powers of the general government. In relation to the power of quelling insurrections, for example, the incidental power heretofore implied, has been limited to that of raising armies, and applying force against insurgents. Yet it would be *very conducive* to the end of suppressing insurrections to prevent them, by establishing good systems of religious and moral instruction. That is a means highly *conducive* to this end, and on the construction of the supreme court would justify congress in taking our schools and churches into their care!—This construction would even give congress a right to *disarm* the people, as nothing is more *conducive* to insurrection, than having the means to make it successful.—The latitude of construction now favored by the supreme court, is precisely that which brought the memorable sedition act into our code. The object of that law was, to prevent sedition by the people, and as *conducive to* that end, all *inflammatory* publications in the newspapers were prohibited!! That law has however been scouted from the American code. Although pro-

---

[8] Vattel, 374, 402.   [9] Ib. 369.

hibiting such publications might be *conducive to* the end in view, it has not *lately* been considered as a direct and incidental power, within the meaning of the constitution.

It is supposed by the court that the word "necessary" is not to be taken in the sense I contended for, because, in another part of the constitution, the term "indispensably" is added to it. If there be any essential difference, between "indispensably necessary," and "indispensably requisite" (one of the meanings of the word "necessary," given by Johnson), I am not able to discern it.

Again the supreme court has said, that congress may use any means "appropriate or adapted to the end." They have not that latitude of power, unless you expunge the word "necessary" from the constitution.

I had intended, Mr. Editor, to enter into a more detailed enquiry as to the constitutionality of the bank of the U. States. That however is but a single measure, and must probably be submitted to. With respect to it, the maximum *"factum valet fieri non debet"* must, perhaps, apply. I would yield to it on the single principle, of giving up a part to save the whole. I principally make war against the declaratory decision of the supreme court, giving congress power to "bind us in all cases whatsoever."—That measure (the bank) has, perhaps, so entwined itself into the interests and transactions of our people, that it may not, without difficulty, be cast off. There is a great difference, too, between *particular* infractions of the constitution, and declaratory doctrines having the effect to change the constitution.—That bank, however, is certainly not *necessary* to the existence of the general government. It is not more so, than the banks of the several states. It may, like the state banks, *refuse* to lend money to the general government.—If with a view to *secure* these loans congress should take the bank entirely into its own hands, it would so augment the powers of the government as to endanger the liberties of the people. The old bank expired before the late war commenced, and the present one was only established since the peace; so that our country got along without it, through a bloody war, against a most powerful nation, and when a band of internal traitors was arrayed against it. After this, can a bank be said to be *essential* to the existence of the country? Russia, Prussia, and other European governments, of high rank, have no banks, nor had England, prior to the period of her revolution. They are, therefore, not indispensable. While this institution is not *necessary*, in relation to the government of the United States, its establishment cuts deep, on the other hand, into the rights of the several states. Among other objections to it, coming under this head, it enables the corporation of the bank by its *by laws*, to *repeal* the laws of the several states (§ 7 of the act establishing the bank;!) a right only given to the *congress* itself, by the constitution, and that only when acting under its provisions. It repeals a right before possessed by the states, to limit the number of banks within their territory. It inundates them with paper money, under pain of submitting to that evil, or breaking their faith with their own banks, previously established. If they should consent to this last alternative, as the lesser of two evils, it obliges them to refund from their treasuries, the premiums they have received therefor. These banks increase usury in the several states contrary to the policy of their laws, not only by permitting them to trade upon perhaps three or four times their capital stock, but by the saving which our banks have been, universally, found to produce. They exempt the persons of the stockholders from imprisonment for their bank debts, and the *other* property of the said stockholders from its liability to pay their said debts, in equal violation of justice, and the laws of the several states. They give exclusive privileges within the states, without any public services rendered to the states therefor, equally contravening a great principle, and the fourth article of the Virginia bill of rights;[10] and they enable aliens and foreigners to hold

[10] "That no man or set of men are entitled to *exclusive* or separate privileges and emoluments from the community but in consideration of public services."

lands, within the several states, in contravention of the general policy of their laws.—The supreme court were pleased to go out of the record, and to tell us, that some of our distinguished functionaries had changed their opinions, on this subject. They forgot, however, to inform us, that a motion was made and *rejected*, in the general convention, to give congress the power of erecting corporations.[11] They also omitted to state, that Washington hesitated on this subject, till the last moment, and then decided, against the *majority* of his cabinet,[12] and particularly against the opinion of Mr. Jefferson.—As to the point of acquiescence, in addition to the few remarks I made before, it is to be observed that only two bills have passed for establishing banks, while[13] two have been rejected. So that the account stands two and two. There was an interregnum, if I may so say, as to this institution. . . . There has been a chasm in the time of its continuance. It has not even that characteristic which is essential to the goodness of a custom, by the common law. It has not been *continued*.[14] This interrupted acquiescence, too, may have arisen from another cause. The contract being made, it may have been supposed, that the public faith required that it should be permitted to have its effect; or to run out.—We are told by Vattel,[15] that the *suspension* of a right does not *abandon* it, for that the suspension may have been prudent. There is no doubt that many of those who voted for the bank, did it under what was supposed the peculiar pressure of the times. It was not adopted in relation to ordinary times, nor on the ground of its being a constitutional measure. I am possessed of facts, on this point, which entirely justify the idea.

Yet this equivocal and interrupted acquiescence has been

[11] See Mr. Madison's speech against the *first* bank law.

[12] In 5 Marshall's Life of Washington, page 293, it is said that Mr. Jefferson and Mr. Randolph, gave written opinions to the president, *against* the bank, and Mr. Hamilton in favor of it.

[13] That rejected by the casting vote of Mr. Clinton, and one rejected by Mr. Madison in the year 1814.

[14] 1 Black. Com. pa. 77.   [15] Vattel, pa. 414.

deemed by the court, in some measure to settle the question!—
There have been also some *sub silentio* decisions upon the subject.
The court, however, well knows, that decisions of this character,
do not *settle* great questions.—No decision is deemed solemn and
final, which is not rendered upon consideration and argument.

I cannot conclude this number, Mr. Editor, without expressing
my regret at another position taken by the supreme court. They
say, that if the *necessity* of the bank was less apparent than it is, it
being an *appropriate* measure, the degree of the *necessity* is to be
exclusively decided on, by congress. If it is only an *appropriate*
means, how does the question of its *necessity* arise? And if congress
should assume a power under a degree of necessity short of that
contemplated by the constitution, ought not the court to interfere?
—Are congress, "although there is a written constitution, to follow
their own will and pleasure"?

June 18, 1819   HAMPDEN

IV

I appeal unto Caesar.[1]

To the Editor of the Enquirer:

I come now to urge my objection to the jurisdiction of the court.
It goes on the ground, that it is not competent to the general government, to usurp rights reserved to the states, nor for its courts
to adjudicate them away. It is bottomed upon the clear and broad
principle, that our government is a *federal*, and not a consolidated
government. I differ entirely from the supreme court when they
say, that by *that tribunal*, alone, can the decision which they have
made be made; and when they further say, that on the supreme
court has the *constitution* devolved that important duty.

I am not able to say with certainty from the *language* of the su-

---

[1] Acts of the Apostles, ch. 25, v. 11.

preme court, whether they aver our government to be a national government, or admit it to be a *federal* one. Two very respectable writers[2] seem to be at issue upon this question, and I shall not undertake to determine the controversy, *absolutely*, between them. Such is the indistinctness of the *language* used by the court that it might not be perfectly easy to do it. On the one hand they use the term *people* in a sense seeming clearly to import the people of the United States, as contradistinguished from the people of the several states, from which the inference would arise, that the states were not known in the establishment of the constitution, and, on the other hand, they admit that the state of Maryland is a *sovereign state*, and a *member* of the general government, and that the *conflicting powers* of the government of the union and of its *members*, are to be settled by the decision. It is not easy to discern how a government whose *members* are *sovereign* states, and whose powers conflict with those of such states, can be a national or consolidated government. These traits indicate, only, a *federal* government: a consolidated government, on the other hand, is one which acts only on individuals, and in which other states and governments are not known. The opinion of the supreme court seems further to incline to the side of consolidation, from their considering the government as no alliance or league, and from their *seeming* to say that a federal government must be the offspring of the state *governments*. On the contrary, I contend, that those governments have no power whatever to make or to alter the constitution, and that if a confederal government can be established at all, it must be by the *people* of the several states, and by them only.

Whatever may be the *language* of the court, however, their *doctrines* admit of no controversy. *They* shew the government to be in the opinion of the court, a consolidated and not a *federal* government. *They* are wholly inapplicable to a government of

[2] "Amphyction" and "The Friend to the Union."

the latter character.—Differing from the court entirely on this subject, I will beg leave to give my own view of it.

The constitution of the United States was not adopted by the people of the United States, as one people. It was adopted by the several states, in their highest sovereign character, that is, by the people of the said states, respectively; such people being competent, and *they* only competent, to alter the pre-existing governments operating in the said states.

We are told by the Federalist[3] that the constitution was founded on the assent of the people of America, but that this assent was given by them, not as individuals composing one entire nation, but as composing the distinct states: and that the assent is that of the *several states*, derived from the supreme authority in each state, that of the people thereof respectively: and that therefore the establishment of the constitution is *not* a *national* but a *federal* act. We are further told in the same page, that its being a federal, and not a national act, is obvious from this, that the ratification results not from a majority of the people of the union, nor even from that of a majority of the states; but that it must result from the unanimous assent of all the states that are parties to it, differing no otherwise from their ordinary assent, than its being expressed, not by the legislative authority, but by the *people* themselves: and that were the people regarded in this transaction, as forming *one* nation, the will of the majority would bind the minority, but that neither a majority of votes, nor of states, has decided. It is again stated in the same book[4] that the states of New Hampshire, Georgia, Rhode Island, Jersey, Delaware, South Carolina, and Maryland, being a majority of the then states, did not contain *one third* of the people of the union, so that a majority of the states were a minority of the people of the union; and that if you even added N. York, and Connecticut (to make *nine*, the number of states necessary to the adoption), the people in them all, would

[3] 1 vol. pa. 257.   [4] 1 Fed. 141.

be still *less* than a majority. If to this fact you add another, namely, that while these nine adopting states might carry the constitution by mere majorities, the non-adopting states might be *unanimously* against it, the portion of the people of America, who, in that case, might adopt the government, would be, indeed, extremely small. This was not, at the time, an extreme or improbable supposition. It was very reasonable to suppose that the people of the great states, would be almost unanimously against a government, which not only vastly extended the sphere of general legislation, but put the small states, in the senate, on an entire equality with themselves. A government adopted by this *fragment* of the people of the United States, could not be justly considered as a *national* government, but as a federal one; the character of which government is, that all its members, however small, are to be regarded as sovereignties, and placed upon an equal footing.

In the convention of Virginia, it was said by Mr. Madison,[5] that the people are parties to the government, but not the people as composing one great body, but as composing *thirteen* sovereignties: that were it the act of the former, the assent of a majority would be sufficient, and that that assent being already obtained (by the previous adoptions of other states), we need not now deliberate upon it. It was said, in the same body, by Mr. H. Lee[6] that if this were a consolidated government, it ought to be ratified by the people as individuals, and not as states; and that if Virginia, Connecticut, Massachusetts, and Pennsylvania, had ratified it, these being a majority of the people, would by their adoption have made it binding on all the states, which not being so, shews that it is not a consolidated government.

So it is stated in the report of 1799, that the powers of the general government result from a *compact*, to which the *states* are parties:[7] and, again, that the *states* are parties to the compact, not in the other senses in which the term "state" is sometimes used,

[5] Debates Vir. Con. pa. 76.   [6] Debates Vir. Con. pa. 135.
[7] Madison's report, pa. 35.

but in the sense of the people of the states, in their highest sovereign capacity, and that in that sense the constitution was submitted to the states, in that sense they ratified it, and in that sense *they* are consequently parties to the compact.[8]

Can it be said, after this, that the constitution was adopted by the people of the United States as *one* people? Or can it be denied that it was adopted by the several states, by the people of the said states respectively, and are *they* not parties to the compact?

The supreme court seems to have laid great stress upon the expression, "We the people of the United States," contained in the preamble to the constitution. This expression does not necessarily import the people of *America*, in exclusion of those of the *several states*. In the last sense it may be justly taken, and thus correspond with the *fact*, as to its adoption. But if this were not so, this declaration in the preamble, would be controlled by the fact of the case. A declaration in the preamble of a deed, that it was executed by three persons, does not make it a deed of them *all*, if it were executed by *two* of them only: and *far less* can it make *that* the deed of A, which was only executed by B. It is not here to be forgotten that the preamble is no part of the constitution. If it were, it would carry to congress all powers which are conducive to "the general welfare;" which is an idea long since exploded.

The opinion of the supreme court would *seem* to import, as aforesaid, that ours is not a federal government because it was not adopted by the *governments* of the several states. The old confederation, I admit, was adopted by the legislatures of the several states: but the validity of that adoption may well be questioned. That adoption took place, in the infancy of our republic, and when we had not emancipated ourselves from the opinion, which still prevails in Europe, that the sovereignty of states abides in their kings, or *governments*. *That* is, in this country, and at this day, an outrageous heresy. None but the *people* of a state, in exclusion

[8] Ib. pa. 36.

of its government, are competent to make or reform a government of whatever nature. The governments are their deputies, for limited and defined objects. It is a principle of common sense, as well as common law, that a deputy cannot make a deputy. The power of changing the government was, therefore, not vested in the state *governments*, but remained with the *people* thereof. To say, therefore, that there can be no *federal* government, unless it be adopted by the *governments* of the several states, is to say, that there can be no *federal* government at all. A *federal* government can be made, as ours was made, by the *people* of the several states, and can be made by none other.

The Supreme Court would, perhaps, infer that ours is a consolidated, and not a federal government from the unequal representation which exists (considered in relation to the several states) in the house of representatives; and from that government's acting, in some instances, directly upon the people. Neither of these circumstances operates that effect, either under the opinions of learned writers on that subject, in general, nor under the authorities particularly applicable in our own country.

As to the first, Montesquieu tells us[9] that the Lycian republic was an association of twenty-three towns, *unequally* represented in the common council, that these towns contributed to the expences of the state, according to the ratio of the suffrages, and that the judges and town magistrates of the several towns, were elected *not* by themselves, but by the common council. That republic was entirely analogous to ours in the first two particulars, and *stronger* in the last; and yet that learned author says, "were I to give a model of an excellent federal republic, I should pitch upon that of Lycia."

This idea of that writer is entirely approved by the authors of the Federalist. After quoting the facts just mentioned, respecting the Lycian republic, and saying of the appointment of the judges

[9] 1 vol. pa. 186.

and magistrates of the respective cities, that it was a most delicate species of interference in their *internal* administration, and which seemed exclusively to belong to the *local* jurisdictions, this work entirely adopts Montesquieu's opinion, and says that the objections founded on those circumstances, and which it entirely overrules, are "the novel refinements of an erroneous theory."[10]

So it is said in the same book (the Federalist) that it is not essential to a *confederacy*, that its authority should be restricted to its members, in their *collective* capacities, without reaching the individuals of whom they are composed.[11] Again, it is said, that so long as the *separate organization* of the members of a confederate republic be not abolished, so long as it exists for local purposes, it would still be in fact and theory, an *association* of states, or a *confederacy*: it is further said, that our constitution, so far from implying an abolition of the state *governments*, makes *them* constituent parts of the national government, by allowing them a direct representation in the Senate, and leaves in their possession, certain exclusive, and very important portions of the sovereign power; and that this corresponds, in every rational import of the terms, with the idea of a federal government:[12] again it is said, that the state governments are *constituent* and essential parts of the federal government,[13] and that the equal votes of the states in the senate, is, at once, a constitutional recognition of the portion of sovereignty remaining in the *states*, and an instrument for preserving it to them.[14] It is said, in another part of the same work, that each state ratifying the constitution, is considered as a *sovereign* body, independent of all others, and only to be bound by its own voluntary act, and that in this relation, the constitution is a *federal* and not a national constitution:[15] and, again, that the states are considered as distinct and independent sovereignties by the proposed constitution.[16] In the same book, while it is admitted

[10] 1 Fed. pa. 54.
[12] Ib. 53.
[14] Ib. 98.
[16] Ib. 264.

[11] Ib. 52.
[13] Fed. 306.
[15] Ib. 257.

that the government has many national traits or features, and is of a mixed character, it is asserted to have *at least* as many *federal* as national features.[17]

In the convention of Virginia, it was said, by Mr. Madison, that the government is of a mixed nature: that in some respects it is of a *federal*, and in others, of a consolidated nature, & that it is shewn to be *federal* by the equal representation in the senate.[18]

The *federal* character of the government is further manifested by the provision (2 § of 1 art. of consti.) that each state is to have *at least* one member in the house of representatives: and this, although its population should fall *below* that of a congressional district. On what other principle is this, than that the states are preserved, and the government a *federal* one?

The court has been pleased to say that no state is willing to allow *others* to control the measures of the general government. If those measures violate the rights of *all* the states, they will be all pleased at it. But this is entirely unimportant. Each state has a *several* interest of its own under the compact, which it is its right and its duty to preserve.

It results from those principles and authorities, that neither by the mode of its adoption, nor in consequence of its having *some* national features, others being purely federal, and the state governments being indispensably necessary to be kept up to sustain that of the union, is our government to be considered a consolidated one. It is a *federal* government, with some features of nationality. The state governments are not only kept up in it, but they are so important that they may actually alter and even abolish the present system. By the fifth article of the constitution, the state legislatures may institute amendments to the constitution, which when reported to & ratified by them, become a part of the constitution. They may thus amend that instrument from the word "whereas;" and thus they may even abolish it. Is it not absurd to say, after this, that this is not a federal government, and

[17] Ib. 258.   [18] Debates Vir. Convention, pa. 76.

that the state governments are not known in it? They can mould and modify the general government at their pleasure, and they can arrest its operations by refusing to appoint senators. The power here admitted to belong to the state legislatures to *amend* the constitution, is no departure from a principle, I have before contended for. These amendments are, in effect, made by the *people* themselves, of the several states. They are made by their legislatures, by virtue of a specific warrant of attorney.

Our general government then, with submission to the opinion of the supreme court, is as much a federal government, or a "league," as was the former confederation. The only difference is, that the powers of this government are much *extended*.

In fact this government may be, in some sense, considered, as a continuation of the *former* federal government. We are told in the Federalist, that "in truth the great principles of the constitution may be considered less as absolutely *new*, than as an *expansion* of the principles contained in the articles of confederation, though the enlargement of the powers is so great, as to give it the *aspect* of an entire transformation of the old government."[19] Again it is said, that the new constitution consists less in the addition of *new* powers, to the government of the union, than in the invigorating of its *original* powers.[20] It was also said, by Mr. Madison, in the Virginia convention, that "the powers vested in the proposed government are not so much an augmentation of powers in the general government, as a change rendered necessary for the purpose of giving efficacy to those vested in it *before*."[21]

If, then, every thing conspires to shew that our government is a *confederal*, and not a consolidated one, how far can a state be bound by acts of the general government violating, to its injury, rights guaranteed to it, by the federal compact? If the founders of our constitution did not foresee these clashings between the respective governments, nor provide an impartial tribunal to de-

[19] Fed. 1 vol. pa. 265.   [20] Ib. 308.
[21] Debates, pa. 188.

cide them, it only affords another instance of the imperfection of the instrument: of which imperfection its authors themselves were most sensible.[22] We are not without a precedent in favor of such a tribunal: for we are told by Vattel[23] that the princes of Neufchatel established in 1406 the canton of Bern the judge and perpetual arbitrator of their disputes; and many other similar instances are there given.

That great writer also tells us, that among sovereigns who acknowledge no superior, treaties form the *only* mode of adjusting their several pretensions, and are sacred and inviolable;[24] and that the faith of treaties form the only security of the contracting parties.[25] It is further said by him, that *neither* of the contracting parties, has a right to interpret the *pact* or treaty, at his pleasure; for that makes *me* promise or *give* whatever *you* have a mind to, contrary to my intention, and *beyond* my real agreement.[26]

In the Federalist, the supremacy of either party, in such cases, seems denied. It is said, in substance, that the ultimate redress against unconstitutional acts of the general government, sanctioned by the authority of their judiciary, there being thus an invasion of the rights of the people, may be redressed by *them*, and that their *state legislatures* will be ready to sound the alarm to the people, and effect a change.[27] Again, it is said, that we may safely rely on the disposition of the state legislatures, to erect barriers against the encroachments of the national authority.[28]— It is further said, in the report of 1799,[29] that an appeal was emphatically made (and not without effect) in the conventions, to the state governments, that they would descry danger, at a distance, and sound the alarm to the people. Another writer entitled to consideration has also said, that in case of infractions of the constitution, by the general government, the state legislatures

[22] As shewn by the provisions for amendment.
[23] Vattel, pa. 44.   [24] Ib. 347.
[25] Ib. 372.   [26] Ib. 370.
[27] 1 Federalist, pa. 300.   [28] Ib. 282.
[29] Madison's Report, pa. 99.

148 ROANE

will sound the alarm; as was done by that of Massachusetts, in relation to what has been called the suability of the states.[30]

In the Virginia convention, it was said by Mr. Randolph, that if congress should attempt an usurpation of power, the influence of the state governments will stop it in the bud of hope;[31] and again, that the *states* can *combine*, to insist on amending the ambiguities in the constitution.[32]

In the celebrated report of 1799 it is stated, as before has been said, that the authority of constitutions is paramount over that of governments:[33] that in case of an infraction of the constitution, the *states* have a right to interpose, and arrest the progress of the evil;[34] and that it is *essential* to the nature of compacts, that when resort can be had to no tribunal superior to the authority of the parties, the *parties* themselves must be the rightful judges, whether the compact has been violated, and that, in this respect, there can be no tribunal above their authority.[35] It is further stated, in the said report, that if this cannot be done, there would be an end of all relief from usurped power, and that the principle on which our *independence* was established, would be violated.[36] It is further said, that the *judiciary* is *not*, in such cases, a competent tribunal, for that there may be many cases of usurpation, which cannot be regularly brought before it; that if one of the parties, in such cases, is not an impartial and competent judge, neither can its *subordinate* departments; and that, in truth, the usurpation may be made, by the *judiciary itself*.[37]—It is further said, that the last resort by the judiciary, is in relation to the authority of the *other* departments of the government and not in relation to the rights of the parties to the compact under which the judiciary is

[30] 1 Tuck. Black. append. pa. 153: and this produced the 11th amendment to the constitution.
[31] Debates, pa. 155.   [32] Ib. 334.
[33] Report. pa. 41.   [34] Ib. 37.
[35] Ib.   [36] Ib. 39.
[37] Ib. 40.

derived;[38] and that on any other hypothesis, the delegation of the judicial power would *annul* the authority delegating it, and its concurrence in usurpation, might subvert, forever, that constitution which all were interested to preserve.[39]

If too, says the report of 1799—pa. 40—if the acts of the *judiciary* be raised above the authority of the sovereign parties to the constitution, so may the decisions of the other departments of the general government, which are not carried before the judiciary, by the forms of the constitution.—This would subject the state rights to violation by the chief *executive* magistrate also, without appeal.

There have been some judicial decisions in full accordance with these principles. In the court of appeals of Virginia, in the case of Hunter v. Fairfax,[40] that court deemed it its duty to declare an act of congress unconstitutional, although it had been sanctioned by the opinion of the supreme court of the United States. It made this decision, on behalf of what it deemed the *reserved* rights of that state under the federal compact. In the state of Pennsylvania, in the case of commonwealth v. Cobbett,[41] the supreme court, with the learned and venerable McKean at its head, resolved in the most explicit terms;—that all powers not granted to the government of the United States, remained with the several states; that the federal government was a *league* or treaty, made by the individual states as one party, and all the states as another; and that when two nations differ about the construction of a league or treaty existing between them, *neither* has the exclusive right to decide it; and that if one of the states should differ from the United States, as to the extent of the grant made to them, there is *no* common umpire between them, but the *people*;—and went

[38] This accords entirely with the principle stated from Montesquieu in my 1st number.

[39] Madison's Report. 40.

[40] 4 Munford's Reports. 58.

[41] 3 Dallas, 342.

on, to render a judgment bottomed on these principles, and in
opposition to the provisions of an act of congress.

The legislature of that state, also, by an act instructing their
senators to oppose the proposed bank law of 1811,[42] has shewn its
entire accordance in these principles. The terms of that act are so
emphatical and appropriate, that I must beg leave to quote a part
of it, in *haec verba*—viz.

In the general assembly of the commonwealth of Pennsylvania. . .
The people of the United States, by the adoption of the federal constitution, established the general government, for *specified* purposes, *reserving* to themselves, respectively, the rights and authorities not delegated in that instrument. To the *compact* thereby created, *each state*
acceded in its character as a state, and is a *party*, the United States
forming as to it, the other party. The act of union thus entered into,
being *to all* intents and purposes a *treaty* between sovereign states, the
general government, by this treaty, was *not* constituted the *exclusive* or
final judge of the powers it was to exercise; for if it were so to judge,
then *its judgment*, and not the constitution, would be the measure of
its authority. Should the general government, in any of its departments,
violate the provisions of the constitution, it rests with the *states* and with
the *people* to apply suitable remedies.

With these impressions, the legislature of Pennsylvania, ever soli-
citous to secure an administration of the federal and state governments
conformably to the true spirit of their respective constitutions, feel it
their duty to express their sentiments, upon an important subject now
before congress—viz.—the continuance or establishment of a bank.—
From a careful review of the powers vested in the general government,
they have the most positive conviction that the authority to grant
charters of incorporation, within the jurisdiction of any state, without
the consent thereof, is *not* recognized in that instrument, either expres-
sively or by *any warrantable implication*. Therefore resolved, by the
said house of representatives, of the said commonwealth of Pennsylvania, in general assembly met, that the senators of this state in the
senate of the United States, be and they are hereby instructed, and the
representatives of this state, in the house of representatives of the
United States, be and they are hereby requested, to use every exertion

[42] See this act in Mr. Leib's speech on that subject.

in their power, to prevent the charter of the bank of the United States from being renewed, or any other bank from being chartered by congress, designed to have operation within the jurisdiction of any state, without first having obtained the consent of the legislature of such state. —Passed both houses, the 11th January, 1811.

I have no knowledge, Mr. Editor, of what may have passed, in other states, on this all important subject. It gives me, however, great pleasure to quote these high acts of the judicial and legislative bodies, of the respectable state of Pennsylvania. That state, great in its population, in its resources, and its devotion to the cause of republicanism, ought to be heard: and its principles and its doctrines accord entirely, with those of the fathers of the constitution.

Of these two judgments of the supreme court of the respectable states of Pennsylvania and Virginia, I may truly say, that they passed on great deliberation, and *unanimously*. I am justified in making this *last* declaration, by the example of the supreme court. For reasons which may easily be conjectured, they have vaunted that the opinion now in question, was rendered unanimously in that court. We hear it also said from another quarter and no doubt with the same view that *some* of the judges who gave it, had before been accounted republicans.[43] If so, their works would lead me to believe that they have changed their politics. In thus changing, they have undergone the common fate attending the possession of power. Few men come out from high stations, as pure as they went in. It is only the elect who can pass, unhurt, thro' a fiery furnace.—We read of a fabled den, in ancient times;[44] from which were seen no returning footsteps—*"nulla vestigia retrorsum."* All the victims were slain as soon as they entered into it. Our judges have met a happier fate; but *if* the information now alluded to, be correct, it would seem that their politics have at least been changed.

How after all this, Mr. Editor, in this contest between the head

[43] The Friend of the Union.   [44] That of Cacus.

and one of the members of our confederacy, in this vital contest for power, between them, can the supreme court assert its *exclusive* right to determine the controversy. It is not denied but that the judiciary of this country is in the daily habit of far outgoing that of any other. It often puts its veto upon the acts of the immediate representatives of the people. It in fact assumes legislative powers, by repealing laws which the legislature have enacted. This has been acquiesced in, and may be right: but the present claim, on the part of the judiciary, is, to give unlimited powers to a government only clothed, by the people, with those which are limited. It claims the right, in effect, to change the government: to convert a federal into a consolidated government. The supreme court is also pleased to say, that this important right and duty has been devolved upon it by the *constitution*.

If there be a clause to that effect in the constitution, I wish the supreme court had placed their finger upon it. I should be glad to see it set out in *haec verba*. . . . When a right is claimed by one of the contracting parties to pass finally upon the rights or powers of another, we ought at least to expect to see an *express* provision for it. That necessity is increased, when the right is claimed for a *deputy* or department of such contracting party. The supreme court is but a department of the general government. A department is not competent to do that to which the whole government is inadequate. The general government cannot decide this controversy and much less can one of its departments. They cannot do it unless we tread under foot the principle which forbids a party to decide his own cause.

While as we are told by Vattel, in a passage formerly quoted, it is often proper for the head and the members of a confederacy to establish an umpire or arbitrator of their disputes, he also tells us that that head is competent to decide the troubles which exist between the several members.[45] The head has not the jurisdiction in the first case, because it is interested; and has it in the second be-

---

[45] Vattel, pa. 44.

cause it is not. The head of the government is entirely disinterested, in relation to the disputes of its members. Our constitution has gone by this principle, in both its aspects. It *has* given to the supreme court, in express terms, a right to decide controversies between two or more states: it has not given to it a jurisdiction over its own controversies, with a state or states. It could not give it, without violating a great principle; and we certainly cannot supply by *implication*, that which the convention dared not to express. In deriving such a power the least that should satisfy us would be an *express* provision in the constitution. If it be said that this power is carried, under the *general* words extending the jurisdiction of the supreme court to "all cases arising under the constitution;" the answer is, that these words may be otherwise abundantly satisfied: they do not *oblige* us to violate the great principle before mentioned. As to this case, the constitution is a law *sub graviori lege*. That paramount law is the great principle I have just mentioned. A constitution giving by these words, a jurisdiction in the case before us, would equally subject the emperor of Russia to the jurisdiction of the supreme court! There is another principle which is also conclusive. The rank of this controversy between the head and one of the members of the confederacy, may be said to be *superior* to those depending between two of the members: and the lawyers well know, that a specification beginning with a person or thing of inferior grade, excludes those of a superior. If in the face of these great principles, this power was intended to be given, would it not have been expressly provided for in the constitution?

I have thus, Mr. Editor, stated to you SOME of the objections I have to the opinion of the supreme court. There are other points in that opinion, equally objectionable. I leave them to abler hands. The objections I have stated, are of overruling influence if they be well founded. I have shewn, or endeavored to shew, that the supreme court has erroneously decided the actual question depending before it: that it has gone far beyond that question, and in an extrajudicial manner established an *abstract* doctrine: that they have established it in terms so loose and general, as to give to congress an unbounded authority, and enable them to shake off the limits imposed on them, by the constitution: I have also endeavored to shew that the supreme court has, without authority, and in the teeth of great principles, created itself the *exclusive* judge in this controversy. I have shewn that these measures may work an entire change in the constitution, and destroy entirely the state authorities. In the prosecution of this plan, it has been deemed expedient to put the state legislatures *hors de combat*. *They* might serve, at least, to concentrate public opinion, and arrest, as they have heretofore done, the progress of federal usurpation. The people of this vast country, when their state legislatures are put aside, will be so sparse and diluted, that they cannot make any effectual head against an invasion of their rights. The triumph over our liberties will be consequently easy and complete. Nothing can arrest this calamity, but a conviction of the danger being brought home to the minds of the people. That people, who, in this country have, heretofore, put down the enforcement of the sedition law, which, in the eyes of the judges, was entirely unexceptionable!: that people who, in England, reversed the infamous judgment in the case of ship-money, and the no less infamous doctrines of Mansfield, on the law of libels, can reverse the judgment now in question. To that authority I appeal. I invoke no revolutionary or insurrectionary measures. I only claim that the people should understand this question. The force of public opinion will calmly rectify the evil. I repeat, however, that I have no sanguine presages of success. Such is the torpor of the public mind, and such the temper of the present times, that we can count on nothing with certainty. It would require more than the pen of Junius, and all the patriotism of Hampden, to rouse our people from the fatal coma which has fallen upon them.

June 22, 1819   HAMPDEN

Marshall's
"A Friend of the Constitution"
Essays

Alexandria Gazette, June 30–July 15, 1819

I

If it be true that no rational friend of the constitution can wish to expunge from it the judicial department, it must be difficult for those who believe the prosperity of the American people to be inseparable from the preservation of this government, to view with indifference the systematic efforts which certain restless politicians of Virginia have been for some time making, to degrade that department in the estimation of the public. It is not easy to resist the conviction that those efforts must have other and more dangerous objects, than merely to impair the confidence of the nation in the present judges.

The zealous and persevering hostility with which the constitution was originally opposed, cannot be forgotten. The deep rooted and vindictive hate, which grew out of unfounded jealousies, and was aggravated by defeat, though suspended for a time, seems never to have been appeased. The desire to strip the government of those effective powers, which enable it to accomplish the objects for which it was created; and, by construction, essentially to reinstate that miserable confederation, whose incompetency to the preservation of our union, the short interval between the treaty of Paris and the meeting of the general convention at Philadelphia, was sufficient to demonstrate, seems to have recovered all its activity. The leaders of this plan, like skilful engineers, batter the weakest part of the citadel, knowing well, that if that can be beaten down, and a breach effected, it will be afterwards found very difficult, if not impracticable, to defend the place. The judicial department, being without power, without patronage, without the legitimate means of ingratiating itself with the people, forms this weakest part; and is, at the same time, necessary to the very existence of the government, and to the effectual execution of its laws. Great constitutional questions are unavoidably brought before this department, and its decisions must sometimes depend on a course of intricate and abstruse reasoning, which it requires no inconsiderable degree of mental exertion to comprehend, and which may, of course, be grossly misrepresented. One of these questions, the case of McCullough against the state of Maryland, presents the fairest occasion for wounding mortally, the vital powers of the government, thro' its judiciary. Against the decision of the court, on this question, weighty interests & deep rooted prejudices are combined.—The opportunity for the assault was too favorable not to be seized.

A writer in the Richmond Enquirer, under the signature of "Hampden," who is introduced to us by the editor, as holding "a pen equal to the great subject he has undertaken to discuss," after bestowing upon Congress in general, and some of its most respectable members in particular, language not much more decorous than that reserved for the judges, says, "The warfare waged by the judicial body has been of a bolder tone and character.—It was not enough for them to sanction, in former times, the detestable doctrines of Pickering & Co. as aforesaid; it was not enough for them to annihilate the freedom of the press, by incarcerating all those who dared, with a manly freedom, to canvass the conduct of their public agents; it was not enough for the predecessors of the present judges to preach political sermons from the bench of justice, and bolster up the most unconstitutional measures of the most abandoned of our rulers; it did not suffice to do the business in detail, and ratify, one by one, the legislative infractions of the constitution. That process would have been too slow, and perhaps too troublesome. It was possible also, that some *Hampden* might make a stand against some ship money measure of the government, and, although he would lose his cause with the court, might ultimately gain it with the *people*. They resolved, therefore, to put down all discussions of the kind in future, by a judicial *coup de main*; to give a general letter of attorney to the future legislators of the union; and to tread under foot all those parts and articles of the constitution, which had been heretofore deemed to set limits to the power of the federal legislature."

Without stopping to enquire whether this ranting declamation, this rash impeachment of the integrity as well as opinions of all those who have successively filled the judicial department, be intended to illustrate the diffidence with which this modest gentleman addresses his fellow citizens, and the just comparison he has made between "the smallness of his means and the greatness of his undertaking;" or to demonstrate his perfect possession of that temperate, chastened, and well disciplined mind, which is so favorable to the investigation of truth, and which so well fits him who instructs the public, for tasks in which he engages, I shall endeavor to follow him, and to notice the evidence and the arguments with which he attempts to justify this unqualified arraignment of all those who have been selected for the great duty of expounding our constitution and our laws.

But before I proceed to discuss the principles for which Hampden contends, I must be permitted to bestow a few moments on some other of his preliminary observations.

After representing the "legislative power" as "every where extending the sphere of its activity, and drawing all power into its impetuous vortex," he adds, "That judicial power, which, according to Montesquieu, is, in some measure, next to nothing," &c., "that judiciary, which, in Rome, according to the same writer, was not entrusted to decide questions which concerned the interest of the state, in the relation which it bears to the citizens;

and which, in England, has only invaded the constitution in the worst of times, and then always on the side of arbitrary power, has also deemed its interference necessary in our country."

I do not quote this passage for the purpose of noticing the hostility of Hampden to those American principles, which, in confiding to the courts, both of the union and of the states, the power, have imposed on them the duty, of preserving the constitution as the permanent law of the land, from even legislative infractions; nor for the purpose of enquiring why he has thought it necessary to inform us that "the judiciary in England has only invaded the constitution in the worst of times, and then always on the side of the arbitrary power." I mean only to mark the unjust and insidious insinuation, that the court had thrust itself into the controversy between the United States and the state of Maryland, and had unnecessarily volunteered its services. "The judiciary," he says, "has also deemed its interference necessary in our country."

If Hampden does not know that the court proceeded in this business, not because "it deemed its interference necessary," but because the question was brought regularly before it by those who had a right to demand, and did demand, its decision, he would do well to suspend his censures until he acquires the information which belongs to the subject; if he does know it, I leave it to himself to assign the motives for this insinuation.

With as little regard to the real state of the transaction, he represents the judges as going out of the case, and giving opinions on extrinsic matter. "The supreme court of the United States," he says, "have not only granted this general power of attorney to congress, but they have gone out of the record to do it in the present question. It was only necessary in that case to decide whether or not the bank law was necessary and proper within the meaning of the constitution, for carrying into effect some of the granted powers; but the court have in effect expunged those words from the constitution."

It is scarcely necessary to say that this charge of "in effect expunging those words from the constitution," exists only in the imagination of Hampden. It is the creature of his own mind. But let us see how he makes good his assertion that the court "has gone out of the record." "It was necessary," he admits, "to decide whether or not the bank law was necessary and proper, within the meaning of the constitution, for carrying into effect some of the granted powers." And how, let me ask, was the court to decide this question?—Does it not plainly involve an enquiry into the meaning of those words as used in the constitution? The court is required to decide whether a particular act is inhibited by certain words in an instrument: yet if the judges examine the meaning of the words, they are stopped by Hampden, and accused of traveling out of the record.—Their construction may be erroneous. —This is open to argument. But to say that in making the construction they go out of the record, may indeed show the spirit in which these strictures originate; but can impose on no intelligent man.

I must also be permitted to remark that, in discussing a question concerning the power of congress to pass a particular act, it is not allowable to assume as a postulate that the interests of the people are necessarily on the side of the state which contests that power, or that the cause of liberty must be promoted by deciding the question against the government of the union.—When the right to call out the militia was solemnly denied, and the right to lay an unlimited embargo was seriously questioned, Hampden himself, perhaps, was not of opinion that the interest of liberty of the public required the decision of those points to be against the claims of the United States. In fact, the government of the union, as well as those of the states, is created by the people, who have bestewed upon it certain powers for their own benefit, and who administer it for their own good. The people are as much interested, their liberty is as deeply concerned, in preventing encroachments on that government, in arresting the hands which would tear from it the powers they have conferred upon it, as in restraining it within its constitutional limits. The constitution has defined the powers of the government, and has established that division of power which its framers, and the American people, believed to be most conducive to the public happiness and to public liberty. The equipoise thus established is as much disturbed by taking weights out of the scale containing the powers of the government, as by putting weights into it. His hand is unfit to hold the state balance who occupies himself entirely in giving a preponderance to one of the scales.

If it be possible that congress may succeed "in seeing the constitution expounded by the *abuses* committed under it;" if "a new mode of amending the constitution" may be "added to the ample ones provided in that instrument, and the strongest checks established in it" may be "made to yield to the force of precedents;" if the time may soon arrive when the constitution may be expounded without even looking into it—by merely reading the acts of a renegado congress, or adopting the "outrageous doctrines of Pickering, Lloyd, or Sheffey:" It is not less possible that the constitution may be so expounded by its enemies as to become totally inoperative, that a new mode of amendment, by way of reports of committees of a state legislature and resolutions thereon, may pluck from it power after power in detail, or may sweep off the whole at once by declaring that it shall execute its acknowledged powers by those scanty and inconvenient means only which the states shall prescribe, and without which the power cannot exist.—Thus, "by this new mode of amendment," may that government which the American "people have ordained and established," "in order to form a more perfect union, establish justice, ensure domestic tranquility, provide for the common defence, promote the general welfare, and secure the blessings of liberty to themselves and their posterity," become an inanimate corpse, incapable of effecting any of these objects.

The question is, and ought to be considered, as a question of fair construction. Does the constitution, according to its true sense and spirit, authorize Congress to enact the particular law which forms the subject of enquiry? If it does, the best interests of the people, as well as the duty of those who decide, require that the question should be determined in the affirmative. If it does not, the same motives require a determination in the negative.

June 30, 1819   A FRIEND OF THE CONSTITUTION

II

I gladly take leave of the bitter invectives which compose the first number of Hampden, and proceed to a less irksome task—the examination of his arguments.

These are introduced by laying down these propositions which he declares to be incontrovertible in themselves, and which he seems to suppose, demonstrate the errors of the opinion he censures.

I do not hazard much when I say that these propositions, if admitted to be true, so far from demonstrating the error of that opinion, do not even draw it into question. They may be all true, and yet every principle laid down in the opinion be perfectly correct.

The first is that the constitution conveyed only a limited grant of powers to the general government, and reserved the residuary powers to the government of the states and to the people.

Instead of controverting this proposition, I beg leave to add to the numerous respectable authorities quoted by Hampden in support of it, one other which, in this controversy at least, is entitled to some consideration, because it is furnished by the opinion he condemns. The supreme court say, "The government (of the United States) is acknowledged by all to be one of enumerated powers. The principle that it can exercise only the powers granted to it, would seem too apparent to have required to be enforced by all those arguments which its enlightened friends, while it was depending before the people, found it necessary to urge. That principle is now universally admitted. But the question respecting the extent of the powers actually granted, is perpetually arising, and will probably continue to arise, as long as our system shall exist."

The supreme court then has affirmed this proposition in terms as positive as those used by Hampden. The judges did not indeed fortify it by authority, nor was the necessity of doing so very apparent; as mathematicians do not demonstrate axioms, neither do judges or lawyers always deem it necessary to prove propositions, the truth of which "is universally admitted."

2d. The second proposition is that the limited grant to congress of certain enumerated powers, only carried with it such additional powers as were *fairly incidental* to them; or in other words, were necessary and proper for their execution.

I will here remark, merely for the sake of perspicuity, that the second branch of this proposition, which seems to be intended as explanatory of the first, introduces I think a distinct idea. The power to do a thing, and the power to carry that thing into execution, are, I humbly conceive, the same power, and the one cannot be termed with propriety "additional" or "incidental" to the other. Under the confederation congress could do scarcely any thing, that body could only make requisitions on the states. The passage of a resolution requiring the states to furnish certain specified sums of money, was not an "additional" or "incidental" power, but a mode of executing that which was granted. Under the constitution, the powers of government are given in terms which authorise and require congress to execute them.—The execution is of the essence of the power. Thus congress can lay and collect taxes. A law to lay and collect taxes, and making all the provisions to bring the money into the treasury, is not the exercise of an "additional power" but the execution of one expressly granted. The laws which punish those who resist the collection of the revenue, or which subject the estates of collection in the first instance to the claim of the United States, or which make other collateral provisions, may be traced to incidental powers. Not to those laws which simply execute the granted power. They are a part of the original grant.

The proposition itself, I am perfectly willing to admit, and should pass it over without a comment as one in no degree controverting the principles contained in the opinion of the supreme court, did I not suppose that some attention to the quotation made by Hampden, might conduce to a more clear and distinct understanding of those quotations themselves, and of their application to the subject under consideration.

The object of making them is, I presume, to show that a general grant of a specific power or thing, does not carry with it those incidents, or those means for giving the grant full and complete effect, which the opinion of the supreme court contends for.

His first quotation from Vattel contains words which might easily mislead a careless reader. "Since," says that author, "a nation is obliged to preserve itself, it has a right to every thing necessary for its preservation. For the law of nature gives us a right to every thing, without which we could not fulfil our obligation; otherwise it would oblige us to do impossibilities, or rather would contradict itself, in prescribing a duty, and prohibiting at the same time the only means of fulfilling it."

Hampden has been caught by the words "necessary," "without which," and "only means," in the foregoing passage, which he has marked in italics or capitals, so as to give them a weight not given by the author, and has inferred from them, and other passages in the same book, that what he denominates the incidental power, is limited to things strictly "necessary," or "without which" the obligation could not be fulfilled; and in no case, he says, "is a latitude allowed, as extensive as that claimed by the supreme court."

The great and obvious error of Hampden consists in this. He

converts an affirmative into a negative proposition. He converts a declaration of Vattel, that a nation has a natural right to do certain things, into a declaration that a nation has no natural right to do other things. But for this, I could not ask a stronger passage to show that the terms on which Hampden relies, are employed in a very different sense from that in which he understands them. "A nation" says Vattel, "has a right to every thing *necessary* for its preservation." Will any man seriously contend that the rights of a nation are limited to those acts which are necessary for its preservation, in the sense affixed by Hampden to the term "necessary"? May it not pass the bounds of strict necessity, in order to consult or provide for its happiness, its convenience, its interest, its power? "The law of nature," says Vattel, "gives a right to every thing without which we could not fulfil an obligation." But does it inhibit every thing else? If it does, then our obligations are sufficiently broad and latitudinous to cover the whole extent of human policy and human action.

"A nation," says Vattel, in the same page, speaking of the destruction of a state, "has a right to every thing which can secure it from such a threatening danger, and to keep at a distance whatever is capable of causing its ruin." There is plainly no difference between that which a nation may do for its preservation, and that which it may do to prevent its ruin. It is a continuation of the same subject; the author means to convey the same sentiment; the change of phraseology is merely casual; and it is obvious that the restrictive terms used in the passage quoted by Hampden, are employed in such a mitigated sense, as to have the same signification with the broader words subsequently used on the same subject. In the whole, the author plainly recognizes the right acknowledged and acted upon by all the world, of a nation to exercise all its foresight, its policy, and its means, for its own security; and of the necessity of resorting to those means, it is the sole judge.

I certainly do not perceive the application of these paragraphs, but they are pressed into the service by Hampden.

We are also referred to a passage in Vattel, which respects tacit or implied engagements. I shall quote it rather more at large than we find it in Hampden.—"Tacit faith," says that author, "is founded on a tacit consent, and tacit consent is that which is deduced by a just consequence from the steps taken by any one. Thus all that is included, as Grotius says, in the nature of certain acts on which an argument is made, is tacitly comprehended in the convention; or, in other words, every thing without which what is agreed cannot take place, is tacitly granted."—Several examples of the rule are then given; as, the allowance of provisions to an army which has stipulated for permission to return home in safety; and the security which is tacitly promised to an enemy who demands or accepts an interview.

I acquiesce implicitly in the rule as laid down by Vattel and by Grotius. I wish to extend tacit consent no farther than to that which is deduced by a just consequence from the steps taken by any one: nor to comprehend, by implication, more in a convention than "is included in the nature of certain acts on which an agreement is made." If the supreme court goes farther, I do not understand their opinion.

The case put by Vattel, and quoted by Hampden, of the grant of a free passage, is one on which I should particularly rely, as strongly supporting that liberal and just construction for which I contend.

The grant of a free passage seems, necessarily, to imply no more than that the sovereign who makes the grant shall remain passive, and to include only "every particular connected with the passage of troops," "such as the liberty of carrying whatever may be necessary to an army, that of exercising military discipline on the officers and soldiers, and that of buying at a reasonable rate every thing that an army may want." Yet it is construed to go much further, and to stipulate for something active on the part of the sovereign making it. "He who grants the passage," says Vattel, "is, as far as lies in his power, to take care that it should be safe." That is, he is not only not to injure, but to protect the army while in his territory.

This is certainly a reasonable construction of the grant; but if the implication be necessary, the necessity cannot be absolute or indispensable.

The case of a grant of a house to one man, and of a garden to another, which could be entered only through the house, is put by Vattel as an example of the *restrictive*, in opposition to the *extensive* interpretation. Hampden cannot mean to give this example as forming a general rule—that construction is always *restrictive*, and never *extensive*; and never even reasonable.

In truth, the only principle which can be extracted from Vattel, and safely laid down as a general independent rule is, that parts are to be understood according to the intention of the parties, and shall be construed liberally, or restrictively, as may best promote the objects for which they were made. For this I refer to his whole chapters on the faith, and on the interpretation of treaties. "The uncertainty of the sense," he observes (b.2. sec. 282), "that ought to be given to a law or a treaty, does not proceed from the obscurity, or any other fault in the expression, but also from the narrow limits of the human mind, which cannot foresee all cases and circumstances, or include all the consequences of what is appointed or promised; and, in short, from the impossibility of entering into the immense detail. We can only make laws or treaties in a general manner, and the interpretation ought to apply them to particular cases conformably to the intention of the legislature and of the contracting powers." "Again" (sec. 283), he says, "we do not presume that sensible persons had nothing in view in treating together, or in forming any other serious agreement. *The interpretation which renders a treaty null, and without effect cannot then, be admitted.*" "*It ought to be interpreted in such a manner as that it may have its effect, and not be found vain and illusive.*" "It is necessary to give the words that sense which ought to be presumed most conformable to the intention of those who speak. If many different interpretations present themselves, proper to avoid the nullity or absurdity of a treaty, we ought to prefer that which appears most agreeable to the intention for which it was dictated."

I trust then Hampden will not charge me, as he has charged the supreme court, with using "*high sounding words,*" when, in his own language, I say that "I take it to be a clear principle of universal law—of the law of nature, of nations, of war, and of reason," that all instruments are to be construed fairly, so as to give effect to their intention, and I appeal with confidence to the authority to which Hampden has introduced us, to support my proposition.

July 1, 1819   A FRIEND OF THE CONSTITUTION

III

I now proceed to enquire how the principles of the common law apply to the case. Although I might cite from that code, examples of the extended construction of the words of a grant for the purpose of implying what is not expressed—as that "by the grant of a house, an orchard, and curtilage, may pass"*—or might cite from it the most complete evidence that the *intention* is the most sacred rule of interpretation, I am content to limit my observations to the phrases quoted by Hampden.

I admit it to be a principle of common law, "that when a man grants any thing, he grants also that without which the grant cannot have its effect;" and, by this word "effect," I understand, not a stinted, half-way effect, but full and complete effect, according to the intention of the parties, and to their mutual accommodation.

* Ch. 5.b.3 Ba. abr. 396 c.b.6 Ba. abr. 3 & 4 statute.

Thus, a right of way over the land of another for a particular purpose, whether given expressly or by implication, is to be so exercised as to effect that purpose completely, with convenience to the grantee, and with as little injury to the landholder as is compatible with the full enjoyment of the right. The same principle is laid down by Lord Coke in the passage also quoted by Hampden.— "For," says that great lawyer, "when the law doth give any thing, it giveth, implied by whatsoever is necessary for the taking and enjoying of the same. And, therefore, the law giveth all that which is convenient; viz, free entry, egress, and regress, as much as is necessary." Hampden says the word "convenient" is here convertible with "necessary." This is true. But it is not less true that the word "necessary" is here convertible with "convenient." Lord Coke uses both words, as they are often used, in nearly the same sense. When so used, they signify neither a feigned convenience nor a strict necessity; but a reasonable convenience, and a qualified necessity; both to be regulated by the state of the parties, and the nature of the act to be done. In this case, according to Lord Coke, the party having ingress, egress, and regress, in order to bring away his own, is not obliged to take it away at once; or before it is ready; he may use a reasonable convenience.

I admit also, "that the incident is to be taken *in a reasonable and easy sense*, and not strained to comprehend things remote, unlikely, or unusual." By which I understand, that no strained construction, either to include or exclude the incident, is admissible; but that the natural construction is the true one. This is "taking the incident in a reasonable and easy sense."

The doctrines of the common law then on this subject, are not at variance with those more general principles which are found in the laws of nature and nations. The rules prescribed by each are subjected to that great paramount law of reason, which pervades and regulates all human systems.

The object of language is to communicate the intention of him who speaks, and the great duty of a judge who construes an instrument, is to find the intention of its makers. There is no technical rule applicable to every case, which enjoins us to interpret arguments in a more restricted sense than their words import. The nature of the instrument, the words that are employed, the object to be effected, are all to be taken into consideration, and to have their due weight.

Although I have demonstrated, as I trust, that the quotations of Hampden contradict, instead of proving the principle he would extract from them, I should not do justice to the subject, were I to dismiss it without further comment.

The difference between the instruments in the examples taken from Vattel, or from the books of the common law; and the constitution of a nation, is, I think, too apparent to escape the observation of any reflecting man.

Take that of an invading army, which, after advancing far into the country of its enemy, stipulates for a safe return home.

The parties to this contract are enemies endeavoring to accomplish the ruin of each other. The contract relates to a single operation, the material circumstances connected with which may be, and therefore ought to be, foreseen, and minutely provided for. There is no reason for including in this stipulation, things which it does not clearly reach. Yet even in this case, the words are so construed as to comprehend more than is clearly expressed, in order to give full effect to the manifest intention of the parties. The same observations apply to the case of an interview between enemies.

So, the cases put in the books of the common law, are, all of them, cases of contract between individuals. Having only a single object to provide for, the provisions respecting that object might be explicit and full. It is not to be supposed that any essential circumstance will be omitted, which the parties intended to include in the grant, and there is consequently the less propriety in implying such circumstance. They are all likewise cases of property; and the terms of the grant cannot be enlarged in favor of one man, without impairing the rights of another.—Yet, even in these cases, we have seen that every thing necessary to give full effect to the grant, every thing essential to the perfect enjoyment of the thing granted, passes by implication. Hampden himself is compelled to admit it to be "a clear principle of universal law"—"That the general grant of a thing, or power, carries with it all those means (and those only) which are necessary to the perfection of the grant, or the execution of the power." And he admits also, that by necessary means, he does not intend "in all cases, a sheer necessity"; which I understand to be equivalent to *an absolute or indispensable* necessity.

It can scarcely be necessary to say, that no one of the circumstances which might seem to justify rather a strict construction in the particular cases quoted by Hampden, apply to a constitution. It is not a contract between enemies seeking each other's destruction, and anxious to insert every particular, lest a watchful adversary should take advantage of the omission.—Nor is it a case where implications in favor of one man impair the vested rights of another. Nor is it a contract for a single object, every thing relating to which, might be recollected and inserted. It is the act of a people, creating a government, without which they cannot exist as a people. The powers of this government are conferred for their own benefit, are essential to their own prosperity, and are to be exercised for their good, by persons chosen for that purpose by themselves. The object of the instrument is not a single one which can be minutely described, with all its circumstances. The attempt to do so, would totally change its nature, and defeat its purpose. It is intended to be a general system for all future times, to be adapted by those who administer it, to all future occasions that may come within its own view. From its nature, such an instrument can describe only the great objects it is intended to accomplish, and state in general terms, the specific powers which are deemed necessary for those objects. To direct the manner in which these powers are to be exercised, the means by which the objects of the government are to be effected, a legislature is granted. This would be totally useless, if its office and duty were performed in the constitution. This legislature is an emanation from the people themselves. It is a part chosen to represent the whole, and to mark, according to the judgment of the nation, its course, within those great outlines which are given in the constitution. It is impossible to construe such an instrument rightly, without adverting to its nature, and marking the points of difference which distinguish it from ordinary contracts.

The case which comes nearest to it, is a treaty regulating the future intercourse between two nations. If in such a treaty "it is impossible from the narrow limits of the human mind," to foresee all cases and circumstances, or include all consequences of what is appointed or promised, if, "from the impossibility of entering into this immense detail," the terms of a treaty must be general, and must be applied by interpretation to particular cases, so as to effect the intention of the parties; how much more impossible is it for a constitution to enter into this immense detail, and how much more necessary is it that its principles be applied to particulars by the legislature.

A still more decisive objection to the exact application of the cases put by Hampden, is, that a rule applicable to powers, which may, strictly speaking, be denominated incidental, is not equally applicable to all the means of executing enumerated powers.

An "incident," Hampden tells us, "is defined, in the common law, to be a thing appertaining to, or following another, as being more worthy or principal;" and is defined by Johnson, to be means falling in beside the main design. In his second proposition, he considers "an incident as an additional power."

I am content with these definitions. In applying them to the subject under consideration, I shall show conclusively that the means by which a power expressly granted is to be executed, would, most generally, be improperly classed with incidental powers.

Congress has power "to raise and support armies." Will any man contend that an act for raising an army of ten thousand men, for appointing the proper officers, for enlisting the troops, for allowing them pay and rations, proceeds from a power *appertaining to, or following* the principal power to raise and support armies? Can such an act, with any propriety, be denominated, "means falling in beside the main design?" or "an additional power?"

Is it not too clear for controversy that such an act would be the direct execution of the principal power, and not of one appertaining to or following it? That it would be the main design itself, and not "means falling in beside it"? That it would be the primary, and not "an additional power?"

Had the right "to make rules for the government of the land and naval forces" not been expressly granted, a law made for that purpose would have rested, for its support, on the incidental or implied powers of congress, and to a question respecting its constitutionality, the doctrines of implication would have applied. But, the constitution having expressly given this power, the law enacting the articles of war is the instrument, or the means by which congress has chosen to execute it. With these means the doctrine of incidents has nothing to do. No court has a right to enquire whether the punishments inflicted by the articles of war are necessary or unnecessary. The means are appropriate, and congress may, constitutionally, select and vary them at will.

So congress has power "to establish post offices and post roads."

The law designating post offices and post roads, with all the provisions relating to that subject, is made in execution of this power. Such laws are the means which congress chuses to employ. But the right to punish those who rob the mail is an incidental power, and the question whether it is fairly deducible from the grant is open for argument. Under the confederation, congress possessed no implied powers, and was therefore unable to punish those who robbed the mail, but was capable of regulating the post office. These regulations were means, not incidents.

Thus too congress has power "to constitute tribunals inferior to the supreme court."

An act constituting these tribunals, defining their jurisdiction, regulating their proceedings, &c. is not an incident to the power, but the means of executing it.—The legislature may multiply or diminish these tribunals, may vary their jurisdiction at will. These laws are means, and the constitution creates no question respecting their necessity. But a law to punish those who falsify a record, or who commit perjury or subornation of perjury, is an execution of an incidental power; and the question whether that incident is fairly deduced from the principal, is open to argument. Under the confederation congress could establish certain courts; but, having no incidental powers, was incapable of punishing those who falsified the records, or committed perjury within those courts.

In the exercise of an incidental power, we are always to enquire whether "it appertains to or follows the principal"; for the power itself may be questioned; but in exercising one that is granted, there is no question about the power, and the very business of a legislature is to select the means. It is not pretended that this right of selection may be fraudulently used to the destruction of the fair land marks of the constitution. Congress certainly may not, under the pretext of collecting taxes, or of guaranteeing to each state a republican form of government, alter the law of descents; but if the means have a plain relation to the end—if they be direct, natural and appropriate, who, but the people at the elections, shall, under the pretext of their being unnecessary, control the legislative will, and direct its understanding?

The distinction then between a power which is "incidental" or "additional" to another, and the means which may be employed to carry a given power into execution, though not perceived by Hampden, is most obvious. I have been the more particular in stating it, not only because his attention to it produces errors which pervade his whole argument, but because also it has led him to the application of language of the most unbecoming as well as unmerited asperity, to the judges of the supreme court. He is excessively displeased with them for not having used the word "incident" when speaking of "means." The term "means," he says, "started up on the present occasion, is not only undefined, but is general; and *guile*," he has permitted himself to add, "*covers itself under general expressions.* Why should the supreme court," he continues, "trump up a term on this occasion, which is equally novel, undefined, and general? Why should they select a term which is broad enough to demolish the limits prescribed to the general government by the constitution?"

All this irritation is excited by the heinous offense of using, when speaking on one subject, words directly applicable to that subject, instead of employing those Hampden chuses to prescribe, but which belong to another, and a totally different subject. All must admit that there are *means* by which a legislature may carry its powers into execution; and Hampden is, I believe, the only man in the United States who will deny that the word *means* expresses that idea more accurately, and with more precision, than the word *incidents*.

It is certainly a piece of information which must surprise if it does not instruct us that the word *means* has been "trumped up on this occasion" by the supreme court, that it is "equally novel, undefined and general," and that it is "broad enough to demolish the limits prescribed to the general government."

These strange positions are not in themselves more curious than the manner in which they are supported. We might reasonably expect to find that this favorite term "incidental," which must be dragged into use, not only where it is appropriate, but where it is inappropriate also, was employed in the constitution, and might thence derive some pretensions to this preference over every other word. It is not however to be found in that instrument—and one would therefore suppose, might be used or rejected with impunity, according to its fitness to the subject discussed.

But Hampden tells us that the terms "necessary" and "incidental" powers "were those uniformly used at the outset of the constitution; while the term means is entirely of modern origin." In support of this assertion he immediately quotes a passage from the Federalist, which contains the word *means*, and does not contain the word *incidental*. "A power," says the Federalist in the passage referred to, "is nothing but the ability or faculty of doing a thing, and that ability includes the means necessary for its execution."

If, instead of this general reference to the terms "uniformly used at the outset of the constitution" we go to particulars, we find the words *incidental* and *means*, employed equally, as either in the opinion of the speaker or writer was best adapted to the occasion.

In the debates in the first congress on the bank bill, we find the opponents of that measure continually using the word *means*—and some gentlemen said "the true exposition of a necessary mean to produce a given end, was that mean without which the end could not be produced."

The friends of the bill also employed the same term. They maintained the sound construction of the clause granting to congress the right "to make all laws necessary and proper" for carrying into execution the powers vested in the government, to be a recognition of an authority in the national legislature to employ all the known usual *means* for executing those powers. They farther contended that bank was a known and usual instrument by which several of them were exercised.

In the opinion afterwards given on this subject by the cabinet ministers, as stated to us in the life of Washington, this term is repeatedly used. The secretary of state and the attorney general, observe in substance, that "the constitution allows only the means which are necessary, not those which are convenient." And, after stating the dangerous consequences of such a latitudinous construction as they suppose was contended for by the friends of the bill, these gentlemen add "therefore it was that the constitution restrained them to *necessary means*, that is to say, to those *means* without which the grant of power must be nugatory."

The secretary of the treasury commences his argument with the general proposition, "That every power vested in a government, is, in its nature, *sovereign*, and includes, by *force* of the *term* a right to employ all the *means* requisite and *fairly applicable* to the attainment of the *ends* of such power."

It would be tedious to cite from this masterly argument, every passage in which we find this word *means*. It is used whenever the occasion requires it. It is used too in all the papers of the day which have fallen within my observation. How then can Hampden justify his assertion that this word is "trumped up" by the supreme court, that it is "novel, undefined, and general?"

The third & last proposition of Hampden is, "that the insertion of the words *necessary and proper* in the last part of the 8th section of the 1st article, did not enlarge powers previously given, but were inserted only through abundant caution."

To the declaration that I do not mean to controvert this proposition, I will only add the following extract from the opinion of the supreme court. "The result of the most careful and attentive consideration bestowed upon this clause is that, if it does not enlarge, it cannot be construed to restrain the powers of congress, or to impair the right of the legislature to exercise its best judgment in the selection of measures to carry into execution the constitutional powers of the government. If no other motive for its insertion can be suggested, a sufficient one is found in the desire to remove all doubts respecting the right to legislate on that vast mass of incidental powers which must be involved in the constitution, if that instrument be not a splendid bauble."

The court then does not give to these words any greater extension than is allowed to them by Hampden.

The three general propositions laid down by this writer as containing those great and fundamental truths which are to convict the supreme court of error, have now been examined. The first is directly affirmed, & the last admitted, in the opinion so much reprobated. The second contains in itself, no principle, which that opinion controverts. Yet the quotations arranged under it, and the aspersions, alike unjust and injurious on the supreme court of our country, which are intermingled with those quotations, have been noticed in some detail, because this was necessary to the correct understanding of this application to the subject under discussion.

July 2, 1819   A FRIEND OF THE CONSTITUTION

IV

In his third number Hampden states those specific objections to the opinion of the supreme court, which are to justify the virulent invectives he has so unsparingly bestowed on the judicial department.

Before noticing these objections, I must be allowed to observe that, in recapitulating what he supposes himself to have established in his preceding numbers, he entirely misrepresents what he has himself attempted to prove.

After stating that the clause containing the words necessary and proper was "tautologous and redundant," he adds, "I have also shown that, in that case, such means were implied, and such only, as were essential to effectuate the power; and that this is the case in all the codes of the law of nature, of nations, of war, of reason, and the common law. The means, and the only means, admitted by them all, and especially by the common law, are laid down emphatically to be such, *without which*, the grant cannot have its effect."

Can Hampden possibly believe that he has even attempted to show these things? Can he possibly have so far misunderstood himself? Or does he shift his ground to impose on his readers? Can he already have forgotten that all his quotations and all his arguments apply to "incidental" or "additional" powers, not to the *means* by which powers are to be executed? Can it have escaped his recollection that, so far from even making an effort to show that by any law whatever, it is "laid down emphatically" that those means only may be used in the execution of the power "*without which* the grant cannot have its effect," he has proscribed the term itself, as one "broad enough to demolish the limits prescribed to the general government by the constitution?" "As one which might cover the latent designs of ambition and change the nature of the general government?" Does he not remember, or does he suppose his readers will not remember, the motives he ascribes to the supreme court for "trumping up this equally novel, undefined, and general term?" I will not retort on Hampden the charge of "*guile*" on this occasion, but I cannot leave him the advantage he claims, of having proved that which he has not even suggested. I have not controverted his real proposition "that the limited grant to congress of certain enumerated powers only carried with it such additional powers as were *fairly incidental* to them." But I utterly deny that when a power is granted, "those means *only* may be used in its execution, *without which* the grant cannot have its effect." I utterly deny that this proposition is maintained in any code whatever. When the attempt to establish it shall be made it will be time enough to show that it is totally unsustainable.

I now proceed to the errors ascribed by Hampden, to the opinion of the supreme court.

The first is that the court has agreed in favor of an enlarged construction of the clause authorizing congress "to make all laws necessary and proper for carrying into execution" the powers vested in the government.

Hampden does not venture to assert in express terms that the court has ascribed to that clause the quality of enlarging the powers of congress, or of enabling the legislature to do that which it might not have done had the clause been omitted. He knows well that such an assertion would have been unfounded, for he says "the supreme court itself admits that these terms were used & only used, to remove all doubts of the implied powers of the national legislature in relation to the great mass of concerns entrusted to it. This is an admission by the court that they were not used for the purpose of enlargement."

Why then does he seek indirectly to impress on the minds of his readers this idea known to himself to be incorrect?

But I will advert to the particular instances of this error, which he has selected in support of his charge.

The first is that the supreme court has said that this clause "is placed among the powers of the government, and not among the limitations on those powers."

That it is so placed, is acknowledged. But the court is supposed to be highly culpable for stating the truth, because it was stated for a purpose which this writer condemns.

To demonstrate that this argument was not used for the purpose, or in the manner alleged by Hampden, it is only necessary to advert to the opinion itself.

The court has laid down the proposition that "the government which has a right to do an act, and has imposed upon it the duty of performing that act must, according to the dictates of reason, have a right to select the means." Having reasoned on this proposition, the court adds: "But the constitution of the United States has not left the right of congress to employ the necessary means for the execution of the powers conferred on the government to general reasoning. To its enumeration of powers is added that of making 'all laws which shall be necessary and proper.' "

The meaning of the court cannot be mistaken. It is that this clause expresses what the preceding reasoning shewed must be implied.

The court then proceeds, "The counsel for the state of Maryland have urged various arguments to prove that this clause, tho' in terms a grant of power, is not so in effect; but is really restrictive of the general right, which might otherwise be implied, of selecting means for executing the enumerated powers."

The court then proceeds to combat these arguments of counsel —and combats them so successfully as to draw from Hampden himself the acknowledgement that "the words prohibit nothing to the general government." "It is only contended," he says, "that they create no enlargement of the powers previously given." Yet after thus explicitly yielding the point which was really in contest, he attempts to turn this total defeat into a victory, by contending that those arguments which were urged to prove that this clause did not restrain the powers of congress were brought forward to prove that it enlarges them, and fails of doing so.

No man, I think, who will even glance at the opinion, will fall into the error into which Hampden would lead him. The court, after reasoning at some length upon the clause, says, "To waste time and argument to prove that, without it, congress might carry its powers into execution, would be not much less idle than to hold a lighted taper to the sun. As little can it be required to prove that, in the absence of this clause, congress would have some choice of means," &c. "This clause," the court adds, "as construed by the state of Maryland, would abridge, and almost annihilate this useful and necessary right of the legislature to select its means. That this could not be intended, is, we should think, had it not been already controverted, too apparent for controversy. We think so for the following reasons: The clause is placed among the powers of congress, and not among the limitations on those powers."

The court proceeds to state several other reasons, to show that the clause could not have been intended by the convention to abridge those powers which congress would otherwise have possessed, and concludes with expressing the entire conviction that it could not be construed "to impair the right of the legislature to exercise its best judgment in the selection of measures to carry into execution the constitutional powers of the government."

Hampden himself refers to that part of this conclusion which assigns to the clause the office of removing all doubt respecting the right "to legislate on that vast mass of incidental powers, which must be involved in the constitution," and approves it. Yet he has mentioned this argument, "that the clause is placed among the powers of congress, and not among the limitations on those powers," as his first objection to the opinion of the court; and he objects to it, not because the statement is untrue, but because the court urged it to establish an enlarged construction, an "extension" of the powers of congress.

I appeal to any man of the most ordinary understanding, when I ask if Hampden can possibly have misunderstood the opinion of the supreme court on this point? If he has not, why has he misrepresented it?

The second reason assigned by the court to prove that this clause could not be intended to abridge the powers of congress, is, "That its terms purport to enlarge, not to diminish the powers vested in the government."

Its terms are, "Congress shall have power to make all laws which may be necessary and proper for carrying into execution the foregoing powers."

I ask, with much confidence, whether these words purport to be words of grant, or of limitation? If the answer must be that they are words of grant, then the court stated them correctly. Hampden cannot controvert this: but he censures the argument, because it was urged to prove an extension of the powers of government. It was not so urged. The court states it explicitly as the second reason for believing that this clause did not *abridge* the powers of congress; and adds "no reason has been, or can be assigned, for thus concealing an intention to narrow the discretion of the national legislature, under words which purport to enlarge it."

Why, again let me ask, why has Hampden thus plainly misrepresented the opinion he condemns?

"The supreme court," he says, "has also claimed such an enlargement, on the ground that our constitution is one of a vast republic, whose limits they have pompously swelled, and vastly exaggerated."

The supreme court has not *claimed* "such enlargement" on the ground stated by this very inaccurate writer, or on any other ground.

After stating truly the extent of our great republic, the court says, "The exigencies of the nation may require that the treasure raised in the north should be transported to the south, that raised in the east conveyed to the west, or that this order should be reversed. Is that construction of the constituiton to be preferred which would render these operations difficult, hazardous, and expensive?" &c.

I refer to this whole paragraph in the opinion; and aver that not a syllable uttered by the court, applies to an enlargement of the powers of congress. The reasoning of the judges is opposed to that restricted construction which would embarrass congress, in the execution of its acknowledged powers; and maintains that such construction, if not required by the words of the instrument, ought not to be adopted of choice; but makes no allusion to a construction enlarging the grant beyond the meaning of its ends. The charge of having "pompously swelled, and greatly exaggerated" the limits of the United States, would be too paltry for notice, were it not to remark, that, even in the most unimportant circumstances, Hampden delights to cast unmerited censure.—The court had said, "From the St. Croix to the Gulph of Mexico, from the Atlantic to the Pacific, revenue is to be collected, and expended, armies are to be marched and supported." And is not the St. Croix our north-eastern boundary? Is not Louisiana bounded by the Gulph of Mexico on the south? Does not our late treaty with England establish a line between the territory of the two governments, to the Pacific? And do we not, independent of our unratified treaty with Spain, claim the mouth of the Columbia, which empties into that ocean?

"The supreme court," says Hampden, "also claimed favor in this particular, on account of the magnitude of the trust confided to the general government."

This charge, like every other, is totally unfounded. The language of the court is, "the sword and the purse, all the external relations, and no inconsiderable portion of the industry of the nation, are entrusted to its government. It can never be pretended that such vast powers draw after them others which are inferior, merely because they are inferior. Such an idea can never be advanced. But it may with great reason be contended that a government entrusted with such ample powers, on the due execution of which the happiness and prosperity of the nation so vitally depend, must also be entrusted with ample means for their execution. The power being given, it is the interest of the nation to facilitate its execution. It can never be their interest, and cannot be presumed to have been their intention, to clog and embarrass its execution."

And I ask if every sentiment here advanced be not strictly true? Congress has power to raise armies. Whatever doubts Hampden may entertain of the propriety of granting this power, can he seriously contend that its execution should be so clogged and embarrassed as that the troops cannot be raised in the manner most economical and most convenient to the people? So congress has power to levy taxes, with this only limitation, that direct taxes shall be proportioned to numbers, and indirect taxes shall be uniform. Does he so construe the constitution as to impose other limitations, or to inhibit congress from raising taxes by the means least burthensome to the people?

But be this as it may, it is most obvious that the opinion does not even hint the idea ascribed to it by Hampden. So far from suggesting that an enlarged construction is to be inferred from the magnitude of the trust, it expressly rejects this inference by saying, "It can never be pretended that such vast powers draw after them others which are inferior, merely because they are inferior."

The argument is plainly advanced by the court in opposition to that unnaturally restrained construction which had been pressed by the counsel for the state of Maryland; and contends only that the government should be allowed, for the execution of its powers, means co-extensive with them.

I ask if Hampden himself can deny the correctness of this reasoning? I ask if he can discern any thing in the proposition that means for the execution of powers should be proportioned to the powers themselves, which contends that those powers ought to be enlarged by construction or otherwise?

July 3, 1819   A FRIEND OF THE CONSTITUTION

V

With as little regard to the text on which he comments as was shown in the instances mentioned in the preceding number, Hampden says, "The court is pleased to remind us with the same view" (that is with a view to a construction that shall extend the powers of congress) "that it is a constitution we are expounding."

He is so very reasonable as not to deny that it is a constitution. Consequently he does not, on this occasion, charge the court with using an inaccurate expression. Its offensiveness consists only in the intention with which it is used.—This criminal intention exists only in the fertile imagination of Hampden. The court makes no allusion whatever to that enlarged construction which he ascribes to it.

In answer to the argument that the clause under consideration so narrowed the powers of congress as to prohibit the passage of any law *without which* any given power could be executed, the court, after showing that the word *necessary* did not always import the last degree of necessity, or that "*sheer* necessity" of which

Hampden speaks, adds, "in its construction, the subject, the context, the intention of the person using it, are all to be taken into view." And I stop to ask if any fair mind can reject this rule of exposition? This "provision," continues the court, "is made in a constitution intended to endure for ages to come—and consequently, to be adapted to the various crises of human affairs. To have prescribed the means by which government should, in all future time, execute its powers, would have been to change entirely the character of the instrument, and to give it the properties of a legal code."

The passage is too long to be quoted entire, but I say with confidence that it does not contain the most distant allusion to any extension by construction of the powers of congress. Its sole object is to remind us that a constitution cannot possibly enumerate the means by which the powers of government are to be carried into execution.

The correctness of this position, Hampden does not venture to deny. He distinctly admits it; but thinks it necessary to add (as if the contrary had been insinuated by the supreme court) "that the constitution establishes a *criterion* in relation to them, and that criterion should be the *law* to the several departments in making the selection."

The whole opinion of the court proceeds upon this basis, as on a truth not to be controverted. The principle it labors to establish is, not that congress may select means beyond the limits of the constitution, but means within those limits.

The grand objection made to the opinion so bitterly inculpated is, that it construes the clause which has been so frequently repeated, as an enlargement of the enumerated powers of congress, and contends, throughout, for an extension of these powers beyond the import of the words. To support this objection, various passages are selected from it. I have reviewed them all; and have, I think, demonstrated that no one of them will bear the construction for which Hampden contends. I do not fear to be contradicted by any rational man who will read the opinion with a real desire to understand it, when I say that it contains not a single sentence in support of these doctrines. In form and in substance, it is a refutation of the argument that this clause narrows the right of congress to execute its powers; and it claims only that, in ascertaining the true extent of those powers, the constitution should be fairly construed.

Why has Hampden attempted thus plainly to pervert this opinion, and to ascribe to it doctrines which it clearly rejects? He knows well that prejudices once impressed on the public mind, are not easily removed; and that the progress of truth and reason is slow.

I should perhaps trespass too much on the patience of the public, were I to advert with the same minuteness to every thing said by Hampden on the subject of the means by which congress may constitutionally exercise its enumerated powers, or to cite from the opinion of the court the several passages to which he alludes with disapprobation, and which he misstates either directly or by insinuation. I have examined them all with attention, and I say, without fear of contradiction, that the general principles maintained by the supreme court are, that the constitution may be construed as if the clause which has been so much discussed, had been entirely omitted. That the powers of congress are expressed in terms which, without its aid, enable and require the legislature to execute them, and of course, to take means for their execution. That the choice of these means devolve on the legislature, whose right, and whose duty it is, to adopt those which are most advantageous to the people, provided they be within the limits of the constitution. Their constitutionality depends on their being the natural, direct, and appropriate means, or the known and usual means, for the execution of the given power.

In no single instance does the court admit the unlimited power of congress to adopt any means whatever, and thus to pass the limits prescribed by the constitution. Not only is the discretion claimed for the legislature in the selection of its means, always limited in terms, to such as are appropriate, but the court expressly says, "should congress under the pretext of executing its powers, pass laws for the accomplishment of objects, not entrusted to the government, it would become the painful duty of this tribunal, should a case requiring such a decision come before it, to say that such an act was not the law of the land."

How then can Hampden justify to his country, or even to himself, the declarations "that the court had resolved to put down all discussions respecting the powers of the government in future, by a judicial *coup de main*; to give a general letter of attorney to the future legislators of the union; and to tread under foot all those parts and articles of the constitution which had been heretofore deemed to set limits to the power of the federal legislature." That in fact "the court had granted to congress unlimited powers under the pretext of a discretion in selecting means?"

In a grand effort to impair the constitution of our country by construction, the doctrine "that the end will justify the means," seems not to be entirely exploded.

Hampden is much dissatisfied with the declaration of the court "that the general government, though limited in its powers, is supreme within the sphere of its action." He "does not understand this jargon. This word supreme," he says, "does not sound well in a government which acts under a limited constitution."

This writer, the least of whose charges against the supreme court is inaccuracy of language, would seem to have confounded *supremacy* with *despotism*. The word "supreme" means "highest in authority"; and there must be a highest in authority under a limited, as well as under an unlimited constitution. Is not the government of the union, "within its sphere of action," "supreme," or "highest in authority"? This is certainly the fact, and is as certainly the language of the constitution. That instrument declares, that "This constitution and the laws of the United States, made in pursuance thereof," &c. "shall be the supreme law of the land." The states, the state judges, and the people, are bound by it, "any thing in the constitution or laws of any state to the contrary notwithstanding." Is not that power supreme which can give the supreme law?

The constitution may be changed, any constitution may be changed. But while it remains what it is, the government "while moving within its proper sphere," is supreme. What authority is above it?

This "jargon" may grate harshly on the ears of Hampden, and he may be unaccustomed to it; but it is the language of truth, and of the constitution, and his displeasure will not banish it. The language of nature and of truth would grate harshly on the ears of an Eastern despot, unaccustomed to its words. He would not like "such jargon." But it would not be, on that account, inaccurate or improper.

In the continued spirit of misrepresentation, Hampden says, "The court is of opinion, that the right to establish a bank stands on the same foundation with that to exact oaths of office"; and also, that "the denial of a right to establish banks" "carries with it the denial of that of annexing punishments to crimes."

I do not deny that the cases bear a strong analogy to each other; but I do deny that the court has made the statement ascribed to it; and therefore, I do not deem it incumbent on me, in this mere justification of a judicial opinion, to show the fallacy of Hampden's distinctions between them, or to prove propositions, however true they may be, which the opinion does not assert.

The counsel for the state of Maryland, we are told, had contended that the clause which Hampden asserts to be "tautologous and redundant," "limits the right of congress to make laws for the execution of the powers granted by the constitution, to such as are indispensable, and *without which* the power would be nugatory."

The court rejects this construction, and in reasoning against it, says, "If we apply this principle to any of the powers of the government, we shall find it so pernicious in its operation, that we shall be compelled to discard it." The court then proceeds to show that this principle, if recognized, would prove many of those acts, the constitutionality of which, are universally acknowledged, such as the act prescribing the oaths of office, &c. to be usurpations. The argument is, avowedly, urged to disprove a proposition supported by counsel in the cause, as all essential in the construction of the constitution, but which Hampden expressly abandons as unsustainable.

He is equally incorrect when he says, "The supreme court is farther of opinion, that the power of incorporating banks is justified by the admitted right of congress to establish governments for the vacant territories of the United States."

The court had shown by a long, and, I think, an accurate course of reasoning, that, "if the end be within the scope of the constitution, all means which are appropriate, which are plainly adapted to that end, which are not prohibited, but consist with the letter and the spirit of the constitution, are constitutional."

But it had been urged that a bank, should it even be a measure of this description, is placed beyond the reach of congress, because the legislature of the union has no power to erect a corporation.

The court proceeds to consider this argument; and, in order to show its fallacy, proves incontestably, that the act of incorporation is the mere annexation of a quality to a measure, to the doing which, if the measure itself be proper, the constitution creates no objection. In illustration of this argument, reference is made to the territorial governments which are corporations. This reference is not made for the purpose of showing that a bank is as absolutely necessary to the union, as a government to a territory; but of showing that if an instrument be proper in itself, the circumstance that an act of incorporation is essential to its efficacy, creates no constitutional objection to it.

After a long and perspicuous review of the arguments which

had been urged against the act of congress which was under consideration, the court proceeds to the act itself, and places its constitutionality simply on the ground, that a bank is "a convenient, a useful, and an essential instrument in the prosecution of the fiscal operations of the government." "That all those who have been concerned in the administration of the finances, have concurred in representing its importance and necessity."

The court may be mistaken in the "propriety and necessity" of this instrument. I do not think so; but others may honestly entertain this opinion. Be this as it may, the grand objection to the opinion, the reason assigned for all the malignant calumnies which have been heaped upon the judicial department, is, not that the court has decided erroneously, but that its decision is placed on principles which prostrate all the barriers to the unlimited power of the general government. That it "has made a declaratory decision that congress has power to bind us in all cases whatsoever."

We had before seen how totally untrue this allegation is, so far as it relies for support on the general reasoning of the court; and we now see how untrue it is, so far as it relies on the particular reason expressly given for the decision. That particular reason is, that a bank "is a convenient, a useful, an essential instrument in the prosecution of the fiscal operations of the government, the importance and necessity of which" is so strong that the best judges of that importance and necessity have concurred in representing it; and the most intelligent original enemies of the measure have admitted it.

Hampden himself seems half inclined to make this admission. He says, "there is no doubt but many of those who voted for the bank, did it under what was supposed the peculiar pressure of the times. It was not adopted in relation to ordinary times, nor on the ground of its being a constitutional measure."

If "the pressure of the times" when this bill passed, rendered it necessary, I am at a loss to conceive how it can be repugnant to that constitution which was made for all times. The peculiar circumstances of the moment may render a measure more or less wise, but cannot render it more or less constitutional.

I have claimed too much of the public attention already, to be equally minute on the remaining observations of Hampden. On his argument therefore respecting the necessity of the bank, I will make only one remark, the correctness of which will be perceived by all who read that argument. He requires that a measure, to be constitutional, must be so indispensable that without it the power cannot be executed. This principle, if at all sustainable, can only be sustained by contending that the clause in which the word "necessary" is found, abridges the powers congress would otherwise have possessed. This construction he has expressly surrendered. He cannot be permitted to avail himself of a construction which he, in terms, abandons.

July 5, 1819   A FRIEND OF THE CONSTITUTION

VI

Hampden has deemed it proper to introduce his objections to the jurisdiction of the court, in the case of McCulloch against the state of Maryland, with a long dissertation on the nature of our government.—On so much of this dissertation as labors to prove that it is not a consolidated one, I will only remark, that it is a truth universally known and universally admitted. No person in his senses ever has, ever will, or ever can controvert it. Any writer who pleases, may certainly amuse himself with the demonstration of this political axiom, but he adds just as much to our political knowledge, as he would to our geographical, were he to tell us, and produce a long train of authorities to prove it, that the United States lie on the western, and not on the eastern side of the atlantic.

But when Hampden says that however "indistinct" may be the language of the court, on this point, "their doctrines admit of no controversy. They show the government to be, in the opinion

of the court, a consolidated, and not a federal government." His
assertion is neither equally true, nor equally innocent.

The question whether our government is consolidated or federal, does not appear to have been stirred in the argument of the
cause. It does not appear to have occurred to counsel on either
side, that any question respecting the existence of the state governments, as a part of the American system, could any where be made.
The motion of such a point would probably have excited not much
less surprize, than if any gentleman had thought proper seriously
to maintain that there was a bench and a bar, and judges on the
one, and lawyers at the other. It is not wonderful then, that the
court should have omitted to state such a question in terms, or
formally to decide it. But the principles laid down, and the language used, presuppose the existence of states as a part of our
system, too clearly to be misunderstood by any person.

The court says, that "the defendant is a sovereign state;" that
"the conflicting powers of the government of the union, and of its
members, as marked in the constitution, are to be discussed;" "that
the government of the union is one of enumerated powers;" "that
it can exercise only the powers which are granted to it;" that "no
political dreamer was ever wild enough to think of breaking down
the lines which separate states, and of compounding the American
people into one mass;" "that the assent of the states in their
sovereign capacity" to the constitution, "is implied in calling a
convention, and thus submitting that instrument to the people;"
"that in discussing the questions" "respecting the extent of the
powers actually granted," "the conflicting powers of the general
and state government, must be brought into view;" "that the
constitution requires" that "the members of the state legislatures,
and the officers of the executive and judicial departments of the
states, shall take the oath of fidelity to it."

If Hampden can reconcile these passages with his assertion,
he will, I doubt not, also reconcile the following: as preliminary
to discussing the right of a state to tax the bank, the court says,

"That the power of taxation is one of vital importance; that it is retained by the states; that it is not abridged by the grant of a similar power to the government of the union; that it is to be concurrently exercised by the two governments; are truths which have never been denied."

The whole opinion is replete with passages such as these. They demonstrate, as conclusively as words can demonstrate, the incorrectness of the assertion, imputing to it the doctrine that the government of the United States is a consolidated one.

Without making, at this time, farther quotations from that opinion, I will proceed to examine the reasons given for the assertions, that this plain language is "indistinct"; & that it conveys "*doctrines*" directly the reverse of what the words import. I shall do so the more readily, because, in treating this part of the subject, this gentleman, though he rarely states correctly the opinion he professes to quote, discloses still more clearly than heretofore, his real sentiments, and real objects; and because those sentiments and that object ought, I think, to receive the most serious attention of the people.

Hampden frequently uses, for what purpose let him say, the word "national" as synonymous with "consolidated." Thus he says, "It is not easy to discern how a government whose members are sovereign states, and whose powers conflict with those of such states, can be a national or consolidated government."

I deny that these terms are convertible. The government of the United States is almost universally denominated the national government, or the government of the nation. It is repeatedly so termed in the Federalist, and in other political treatises, and has never been termed a consolidated government.

Hampden defines a consolidated government to be "one which acts only on individuals, and in which other states and governments are not known." What name will he give us for a government "which acts only on individuals," but "in which other states and governments are known?" Such is the government of the

United States; and, in a work* now acknowledged by all to be a clear and a just exposition of the constitution, we are told, that, according to the definitions of those terms given by its opponents, "it is neither a national, nor a federal constitution; but a composition of both."

But waiving, for the present, any controversy about terms, I will proceed to the evidence adduced in support of the charge that the language of the court, on the question of consolidation, is indistinct.

The first is, that "They use the word *people* in a sense seeming clearly to import the people of the United States, as contradistinguished from the people of the several states; from which the inference would arise, that the states were not known in the establishment of the constitution."

As no particular passage in the opinion is referred to, it is not in my power, by quoting the words of the court, to give a precise refutation to this allegation. I must content myself with the more general, and less pointed observations.

The counsel for the state of Maryland, we are told, contended that the constitution was the act of sovereign states, as contradistinguished from the people. In opposition to this proposition, the court maintained that the constitution is not the act of the state governments, but of the people of the states. In the course of this argument, the term—*the people*—without any annexation, is frequently used; but never in a sense excluding the idea that the people were divided into distinct societies, or indicating the non-existence of states. It is positively denied that this use of the term, even unaccompanied by those passages with which the opinion abounds, would afford any countenance to the inference "that the states were not known in the establishment of the constitution." Still less can such an inference arise in opposition to the express and repeated declarations of the court.

* Federalist, No. 39.

If instead of using the word *"people"* generally, and in a sense avowedly contradistinguished from their governments, the court had used the words *"people of the United States,"* not even this language would have had any tendency to warrant the inference which is said to arise.

Will Hampden deny that there is such a people as the people of the United States? Have we no national existence? We were charged by the late emperor of France with having no national character, or actual existence as a nation; but not even he denied our theoretical or constitutional existence. If congress declares war, are we not at war as a nation? Are not war and peace national acts? Are not all the measures of the government national measures? The United States is a nation; but a nation composed of states in many, though not in all, respects, sovereign. The people of these states are also the people of the United States. The two characters, so far from being incompatible with each other, are identified. This is the language of the constitution. In that instrument, the people of the states term themselves "the people of the United States." A senator must have been nine, a representative seven years "a citizen of the United States." "No person except a natural born citizen, or a citizen of the United States at the time of the adoption of the constitution," is eligible to the office of president. The oath taken by every adopted citizen, is as a citizen of the United States; and we are all citizens, not only of our particular states, but also of this great republic.

The constitution then does not recognize, but rejects, this incompatibility of our existence and character as a nation, with the existence of the several states.—Hampden himself says that the words, "we the people of the United States," in the constitution, "do not necessarily import the people of *America*, in exclusion of those of the *several states*." And I insist that, so far from excluding, they include, "those of the several states." Surely then the term "the people," used generally by the supreme court, and expressly applied to the people acting in their several states, cannot justify the inference "that the states were not known in the establishment of the constitution."

"The opinion of the supreme court," says Hampden, "seems farther to incline to the side of consolidation, from their considering the government as no alliance or league, and from their seeming to say that a federal government must be the offspring of state governments."

I admit explicitly that the court considers the constitution as a government, and not "a league." On this point I shall make some farther observations hereafter. But I deny "their seeming to say that a federal government must be the offspring of state governments." They have expressly said the very reverse. In answer to the argument, that the people "had already conferred all the powers of government on the state authorities, and had nothing left to give," the court says, "much more might the legitimacy of the general government be doubted, had it been created by the states." When Hampden contends that state governments had no power to change the constitution, and represents himself as opposing, in this respect, the opinion he condemns, he is in fact reurging the very argument which had been previously advanced in that opinion. "The powers delegated to the state sovereignties," says the court, "were to be exercised by themselves, not by a distinct independent sovereignty created by themselves."

July 6, 1819   A FRIEND OF THE CONSTITUTION

VII

I proceed now to those doctrines, which, according to Hampden, "show the government to be, in the opinion of the court, a consolidated, and not a federal government."

"Differing from the court entirely," he says, "on this subject, he will give his own view of it."

We must, of course, suppose his view to be in proportion to that from which he differs.

In stating this difference, he tells us, "The constitution of the United States was not adopted by the people of the United States as one people, it was adopted by the several states," &c. And he then proceeds to show that the constitution was adopted by the people of the several states acting in separate conventions.

This is precisely what the court had previously said. It is to be recollected that the question discussed by the court, was, not whether the constitution was the act of the people in mass, or in states; but whether it was the act of the people, or of the state governments? In discussing this question, the court says, "The constitution was reported to the then existing congress of the United States, with a request that it might be submitted to a convention of delegates, chosen in each state by the people thereof, under the recommendation of its legislature, for their assent and ratification. This mode of proceeding was adopted."

Language, I think, cannot be more explicit than this; nor more entirely repugnant to the idea that the people acted in one body, and not by states.

Hampden also alleges in support of this plain perversion of the language and meaning of the court, the stress laid on the words "We, the people of the United States," in the preamble of the constitution.

The opinion cannot be inspected without perceiving that these words are not quoted, as "importing" in the constitution, "the people of America in exclusion of those of the *several* states," but as importing the people, in exclusion of their governments.

The court then has not denied, but has affirmed, that the constitution was adopted by the people acting as states.

Were it even otherwise, this error respecting the origin of the government, would not have proved it "to be in the opinion of the court, a consolidated, and not a federal government."

The character of a government depends on its constitution; not on its being adopted by the people acting in a single body, or in single bodies. The kingdom of Great Britain and Ireland is a consolidated kingdom. Yet it formerly consisted of three distinct kingdoms—England, Scotland, & Ireland; and this union was effected by their several parliaments, acting separately in each kingdom.

The convention of France, which was assembled in 1792, consisted of a single body elected by the people of the whole nation. Had the faction of the Gironde prevailed, and a federal republic been established, it would not have been the less a federal republic, because it was adopted by the representatives of the whole people, acting in mass.

If then the judges had made the assertion ascribed to them, they would have advanced a doctrine equally untrue and absurd, but not one which would "show that, in their opinion, our government is consolidated, and not federal."

The fact alleged then, and the conclusion drawn from it, are equally erroneous.

Hampden states many arguments which he supposes the court might urge in favor of consolidation, all of which he ingeniously refutes; but as the court has not itself urged one of these arguments, and has not, in the most distant manner, suggested a single idea in favor of consolidation, I shall be excused for passing them over without a comment.

I cannot, however, pass over, in like manner, his idea that the ligament which binds the states together, is "an alliance, or a league."

This is the point to which all his arguments tend. To establish this fundamental principle, an unnatural or restricted construction of the constitution is pressed upon us, and a fair exercise of the powers it confers, is reviled as an infraction of state rights. We need no longer be surprized at finding principles supported which would reduce the constitution to a dead letter, at the irritation excited by a course of reasoning which puts down those principles, at the effort to render the terms *American people* and *national government*, odious; at hearing that the supremacy of the whole within its sphere of action, over the parts is "jargon"; or at the exaggerated description of the power of the states to make amendments. All this is the necessary consequence of the doctrine that the constitution is not a national government, but a league, or a contract of alliance between the states, sovereign and independent.

But our constitution is not a league. It is a government; and has all the constituent parts of a government. It has established legislative, executive, and judicial departments, all of which act directly on the people, not through the medium of the state governments.

The confederation was, essentially, a league; and congress was a corps of ambassadors, to be recalled at the will of their masters. This corps could do nothing but declare war or make peace. They could neither carry on a war nor execute the articles of peace. They had a right to propose certain things to their sovereigns, and to require a compliance with their resolution; but they could, by their own power, execute nothing. A government, on the contrary, carries its resolutions into execution by its own means, and ours is a government. Who ever heard of sovereigns in league with each other, whose agents assembled in congress, were authorized to levy or collect taxes on their people, to shut up and open ports at will, or to make any laws and carry them into execution? Who ever heard of sovereigns taking the oath of fidelity to their agents? Who ever heard of sovereigns in league with each other, stripping themselves of all the important attributes of sovereignty, and transferring those attributes to their ambassadors?

The people of the United States have certainly a right, if they choose to exercise it, to reduce their government to a league. But let them act understandingly. Let them not be impelled to destroy the constitution, under the pretext of defending state rights from invasion. Let them, before they proceed too far in the course they are invited to take, look back to that awful and instructive period of our history which preceded the adoption of our constitution. These states were then truly sovereign, and were bound together only by a league. Examine with attention, for the subject deserves all your attention, the consequences of such a system. They are truly depicted in the Federalist, especially in the 15th No. of that work. The author thus commences his catalogue of the ills it had brought upon us— "We may indeed, with propriety, be said to have reached almost the last stage of national humiliation. There is scarcely any thing that can wound the pride, or degrade the character, of an independent people, which we do not experience." And he concludes his long and dark detail of those ills with saying,—"To shorten an enumeration of particulars which can afford neither pleasure nor instruction, it may in general be demanded, what indication is there of national disorder, poverty, and insignificance, that could befall a community so peculiarly blessed with natural advantages as we are, which does not form a part of the dark catalogue of our public misfortunes."

Such was the situation to which these states were brought, in four years of peace, by their league. To change it into an effective government, or to fall to pieces from the weight of its constituent parts, & the weakness of its cement, was the alternative presented to the people of the United States. The wisdom and patriotism of our country chose the former. Let us not blindly and inconsiderately replunge into the difficulties from which that wisdom and that patriotism have extricated us.

July 9, 1819   A FRIEND OF THE CONSTITUTION

VIII

The last accusation brought against the supreme court, is, a violation of the constitution, by deciding a cause not within its jurisdiction.

Grave as is this charge, the question is still more important to the people than to the judges. It more deeply concerns the prosperity of the union, the due execution of its laws, and even its preservation, that its courts should possess the jurisdiction Hampden denies them, than it does the character of the judges, to stand acquitted of usurpation.

Before I proceed to examine this question, I must be allowed to express some surprize at its not having occurred to the counsel for the state of Maryland. The talents of those gentlemen are universally acknowledged; and, if we may judge of their zeal by the specimens of their arguments given in the opinion of the court, they made every point which judgment, ingenuity, or imagination could suggest, on which a decent self respect would permit them to insist. How happened it, then, that this point of jurisdiction escaped them?

A brief consideration of the subject will, I am persuaded, solve this difficulty.

The reasoning on which this objection seems to be founded, proceeds from the fundamental error, that our constitution is a mere league, or a compact, between the several state governments, and the general government. Under the influence of this unaccountable delusion, he makes some quotations from Vattel, favorable to the choice of a foreign government as an umpire to decide controversies which may arise between the government of the union and those of the states. "The princes of Neufchatel," we are informed, "established in 1406, the canton of Berne, the judge and perpetual arbitrator of their disputes."

Were the petty princes of Neufchatel united under one paramount government having a constitutional power to adjust their differences, or were they only in alliance with each other? Was there any analogy between their situation and that of the United States? This at least ought to be shown by him who holds up to us their example for imitation.

He tells us also, on the same authority, "that among sovereigns who acknowledge no superior, treaties form the only mode of adjusting their several pretensions;" and "that *neither* of the contracting parties has a right to interpret the *pact* or treaty, at his pleasure."

There is no difficulty in admitting this doctrine. The only difficulty consists in discerning its application to the United States. It applies to independent sovereigns, who stand in no relation to each other, but that which is created by the general law of nations, and by treaty.—Has Hampden succeeded in convincing his fellow citizens that this is the condition of the American states?

Without pressing further the total inapplicability of these historical facts, and general principles, to our situation; or urging the weakness and danger of introducing into our system, a foreign potentate as the arbiter of our domestic disputes, I will proceed to examine the question of jurisdiction on its real grounds.

I will premise that the constitution of the United States is not an alliance, or a league, between independent sovereigns; nor a compact between the government of the union, and those of the states; but is itself a government, created for the nation by the whole American people, acting by convention assembled in and for their respective states. It does not possess a single feature belonging to a league, as contradistinguished from a government. A league is formed by the sovereigns who become members of it; our constitution is formed by the people themselves, who have adopted it without employing, in that act, the agency of the state legislatures. The measures of a league are carried into execution by the sovereigns who compose it; the measures of our national government are carried into execution by itself, without requiring the agency of the states. The representatives of sovereigns in league with each other, act in subordination to those sovereigns, and under their particular instructions; the government of the union, "within its sphere of action," is "supreme"; and, although its laws should be in direct opposition to the instructions of every state legislature in the union, they are "the supreme law of the land, any thing in the constitution or laws of any states to the contrary notwithstanding." This government has all the departments, and all the capacities for performing its various functions, which a free people is accustomed to bestow on its government. It is not then, in any point of view, a league.

As little does it resemble a compact between itself and its members.

A contract is "an agreement on sufficient consideration to do or not to do a particular thing."

There must be parties. These parties must make an agreement, and something must proceed to and from each.

The government of the United States can certainly not be a party to the instrument by which it was created. It cannot have been concerned in making that by which it was brought into existence.

Neither have the state governments made this instrument. It is the act of the people themselves, and not the act of their governments.

There is then no agreement formed between the government of the United States and those of the states. Our constitution is not a compact. It is the act of a single party. It is the act of the people of the United States, assembling in their respective states, and adopting a government for the whole nation. Their motives for this act are assigned by themselves. They have specified the objects they intended to accomplish, and have enumerated the powers with which those objects were to be accomplished.

All arguments founded on leagues and compacts, must be fallacious when applied to a government like this. We are to examine the powers actually conferred by the people on their government; and the capacities bestowed upon it for the execution of those powers.

This government possesses a judicial department; which, like the others, is erected by the people of the United States. It is not a partial, local tribunal, but one which is national.

For what purpose was this department created?

Before we look into the constitution for an answer to this question, let any reasonable man ask himself what must have been the primary motive of a people forming a national government for endowing it with a judicial department? Must it not have been the desire of having a tribunal for the decision of all national questions? If questions which concern the nation might be submitted to the local tribunals no motive could exist for establishing this national tribunal. Such is the language of reason. What is the language of the constitution?

"The judicial power shall extend to all cases in law and equity, arising under this constitution, the laws of the United States, & treaties made or to be made under their authority."

Cases then arising under the constitution, and under the laws and treaties of the U. States, are, as was to be expected, the objects which stood first in the mind of the framers of the constitution.

Is the case of M'Cullough against the state of Maryland of this description?

Only two points appear to have been made by the defendant in the argument.

1st. That the act of congress establishing the bank is unconstitutional and void.

2d. That the act of the legislature of Maryland is constitutional, and consequently obligatory.

It was then a case arising under the constitution. Let us hear how Hampden contrives to withdraw it from the jurisdiction of the court.

He relies first on certain authorities which he quotes as being favorable to his opinion. In the Federalist, he says, "the supremacy of either party in such cases" ("these clashings between the respective governments") "seems to be denied."

If he seems to say no more than that the positive supremacy of an act of Congress, until it shall be tried by the standard of the constitution, is denied, he is undoubtedly correct. But the application of this opinion to the jurisdiction of the court cannot readily be perceived.

If he means to say that the jurisdiction or the supremacy of the judicial department, in cases of this description, "seems to be denied" by the Federalist, he is as certainly incorrect.

The writers of that valuable treatise allow a concurrent jurisdiction in such cases, except so far as that of the state courts may be restrained by congress; but the supremacy of the courts of the United States, is expressly recognized. In the 80th No. they are full and explicit to the point, that the courts of the Union have, and ought to have jurisdiction, in all cases, arising under the constitution and laws of the United States. After laying down as political axioms, the propositions that the judicial department should be co-extensive with the legislative, and with the provisions of the constitution, the Federalist says "thirteen independent courts of final jurisdiction over the same causes, arising upon the same laws, is a hydra in government from which nothing but contradiction and confusion can proceed."

Still less may be said in regard to the other point. Controversies between the nation and its members, or citizens, can only be properly referred to the national tribunals.

In the 82d No. speaking of the concurrent jurisdiction of the different courts, he adds, "here another question occurs—what relation would subsist between the national and state courts, in these instances of concurrent jurisdiction? I answer that an appeal would certainly lie to the supreme court of the United States." The writer then proceeds to give his reasons for this opinion.

It is then most certain that the Federalist, does not "seem to deny," but does expressly affirm, that the jurisdiction and supremacy of the courts of the United States, [exist] in "all cases arising under the constitution;" which jurisdiction may be applied in the appellate form to those decided in the state courts.

Hampden refers also to two judicial decisions, which, he says, "are in full accordance with his principles." These are the case of Hunter *v*. Fairfax, and the case of the commonwealth of Pennsylvania *v*. Cobbett. In the first case he says the court of appeals of Virginia declared "an act of congress unconstitutional, although it had been sanctioned by the opinion of the supreme court of the United States."

This is true; and it is the only example furnished by any court in the union of a sentiment favorable to that "hydra in government, from which," says the Federalist, "nothing but contradiction and confusion can proceed." But it is also true that this decision was reversed by the unanimous opinion of the supreme court, and has, notwithstanding the acknowledged respectability of the court of appeals of Virginia, been disapproved by every state court, and they are not a few, which has had occasion to act on the subject. The supreme court, as we perceive in the reports, has reversed the decisions of many state courts founded on laws supported by a good deal of state feeling. In every instance, except that of Hunter and Fairfax, the judgment of reversal has been acquiesced in, and the jurisdiction of the court has been recognized. If the most unequivocal indications of the public sentiment may be trusted, it is not hazarding much to say, that, out of Virginia, there is probably not a single judge, nor a single lawyer of eminence, who does not dissent from the principles laid down by the court of appeals in Hunter and Fairfax.

Hampden's representation of the case of the commonwealth and Cobbett is entirely inaccurate. In that case, the supreme court of Pennsylvania did not come to the resolutions he recapitulates, nor, "go on to render a judgment bottomed on those principles, and in opposition to the provisions of an act of congress."

The case, as reported in the 3d Dal. is this:—Cobbett had been guilty of an offense against the criminal code of Pennsylvania, and had been bound in a recognizance to be of good behaviour. His recognizance having been put in suit, he endeavored to remove the cause into the federal court on an affidavit that he was an alien. This motion was opposed, not on the unconstitutionality of the act of congress, but on its construction. The counsel for the commonwealth contended that the case was not within the act,—1st because it gave the circuit court no jurisdiction in a cause where a state was a party; and 2dly because it was not, properly speaking, "a civil suit;" but was incidental to, and in the nature of, a criminal action.

On these grounds the court decided that the act of congress did not embrace the case.

When the decision was about to be made, chief justice McKean, who was, not long afterwards, elected governor of Pennsylvania, whether in his character as a candidate or a judge, I submit to every intelligent reader, thought proper to deliver a political disquisition on the constitution of the United States. "Previous to the delivery of my opinion," he says "in a cause of so much importance, as to the consequences of the decision, I will make a few preliminary observations on the constitution and laws of the United States of America." He then proceeds with the political disquisition stated by Hampden. But this is so far from being a part of the opinion of the court, that it was neither understood, nor stated, even by himself, as belonging in any manner to the cause. After having finished this dissertation, he says, "I shall now consider the case before us." The opinion of the court is then delivered, in which not one syllable indicating the unconstitutionality of the act of congress is to be found. It was held not to comprehend the case.

This decision then, so far from questioning the validity of an act of congress, clearly recognizes its authority. The construction given to the act was, I presume, tho't correct by Mr. Cobbett's counsel, or he would have brought the question before the Federal courts.

July 14, 1819   A FRIEND OF THE CONSTITUTION

IX

Hampden is not more successful in his reasoning against the jurisdiction of the court, than in his authorities.

Having finished his quotations, he exclaims,—How after all this, in this contest between the head, and one of the members of our confederacy, in this vital contest for power between them, can the supreme court assert its exclusive right to determine the controversy?

The court has itself answered this question. It has said—"On the supreme court of the United States, has the constitution of our country devolved this important duty."

Such a question cannot assume a form for judicial investigation, without being "a case arising under the constitution;" and to "all" such cases "the *judicial power*" is expressly extended. The right asserted by the court, is then, expressly given by the great fundamental law which unites us as a nation.

If we were now making, instead of controversy, a constitution, where else could this important duty of deciding questions which grow out of the constitution, and the laws of the union, be safely or wisely placed? Would any sane mind prefer to the peaceful and quiet mode of carrying the laws of the union into execution by the judicial arm, that they should be trampled under foot, or enforced by the sword?—That every law of the United States should be resisted with impunity, or produce a civil war? If not, what other alternative presents itself? Hampden suggests the arbitration of some foreign potentate—Britain, France, or Russia, for example. Is he sure that the parties could agree on an arbiter? Is he sure that such arbiter would be influenced entirely by the principles of right and not at all by those of policy? Is he sure that such arbiter would understand the constitution and laws of the United States? Is he sure that this intrusion of a foreign potentate into our domestic "vital contests for power" would not give that potentate an undue influence over the weaker party, and lead to intrigues which might foment divisions, animate discord, and finally produce dismemberment? If he is not certain on these and many other points which suggest themselves, and ought to be considered, how can he think the submission of these controversies to such an arbiter, preferable to the submission of them to a domestic tribunal, composed of American citizens, selected by the man in whom the American people have reposed their highest confidence, approved by the representatives of the state sovereignties, and placed by the people themselves in a situation which exempts them from all undue influence?

But this is not now a question open for consideration. The constitution has decided it.

After expressing some doubts respecting the propriety of that great American principle, the judicial right to decide on the supremacy of the constitution, a right which is inseparable from the idea of a paramount law, a written constitution, he adds, "but the present claim on the part of the judiciary is to give unlimited powers to a government only clothed by the people with those which are limited. It claims the right, in effect, to change the government, to convert a federal into a consolidated government."

Hampden leaves us to search for that part of the opinion in which this claim is asserted. Is it in the following?—"This government is acknowledged by all to be one of enumerated powers. The principle that it can exercise only the powers granted to it, would seem too apparent," &c.

If not in this, or in such as this, for the opinion abounds with them, is it inseparable from the power of deciding in a last resort, all questions "arising under the constitution and laws" of the United States? If he contends that it is, I answer that the constitution has expressly given the power, and the exercise of it cannot be the assertion of a right to change that instrument.

Hampden again demands the clause in the constitution which grants this jurisdiction. "The necessity," he says, "of showing an express provision for a right claimed by one of the contracting parties to pass finally on the rights or powers of another" "is increased when the right is claimed for a deputy or department of such contracting party. The supreme court is but a department of the general government."

I am not sure that I comprehend the meaning of these sentences. The words "one of the contracting parties" and "general government," appear to be used in the same sense, as designating the same object. So the words "deputy" and "department of such contracting party." If they are not to be understood so, I am unable to construe them. If they are, then let me ask what is meant by the word "general government"? Is it Congress? Is it the whole government? If the former, whence does he derive his authority for saying that the judicial department is the "deputy" of congress? Certainly, not from the constitution. According to that instrument, the judicial, is a co-ordinate department, created at the same time, and proceeding from the same source, with the legislative and executive departments.

If the latter, the whole government consists of departments. Neither of these is the deputy of the whole, or of the other two. Neither can perform the duties, or exercise the powers assigned to another; nor can all of them together participate in those duties and powers, or perform them jointly. Each is confined to the sphere of action prescribed to it by the people of the United States, and within that sphere, performs its functions alone. The legislature and executive can no more unite with the judiciary in deciding a cause, than the judiciary can unite with them in making a law, or appointing a foreign minister. On a judicial question then, the judicial department is the government, and can alone exercise the judicial power of the United States.

Can Hampden have been so inattentive to the constitution of his country as not to have made these observations; or does his hostility to this department lead him to indulge in expressions which his sober judgment must tell him are totally misapplied?

But he denies that there exists in the government a power to decide this controversy. He says—"They cannot do it unless we tread under foot the principle which forbids a party to decide his own cause."

Let us temperately examine how far this principle applies to the case.

The government of the Union was created by, and for, the people of the United States. It has a department in which is vested its whole legislative power, and a department in which is vested its whole judicial power. These departments are filled by citizens of the several states.

The propriety and power of making any law which is proposed must be discussed in the legislature before it is enacted. If any person to whom the law may apply, contests its validity, the case is brought before the court. The power of Congress to pass the law is drawn into question. But the courts of the union, Hampden says, cannot decide this question "without treading under foot the principle that forbids a man to decide his own cause."

What would be the condition of the world should this principle be deemed applicable to the exercise of the judicial authority by the regular tribunals of the country?

An individual of Virginia, for example, chooses to deny the validity of a law, and proceedings for its enforcement are instituted. But, according to this new doctrine the court of the state is incapable of deciding a question involving the power of the legislature, without treading under foot this sacred principle. Let the state itself be a nominal party as in prosecutions for crimes, or suits against its debtors, and the violation of the sacred principle would be still more apparent. How are these questions to be settled without the intervention of a court? Or are they to remain forever suspended?

It is the plain dictate of common sense, and the whole political system is founded on the idea, that the departments of government are the agents of the nation, and will perform, within their respective spheres, the duties assigned to them.—The whole owes to its parts the peaceful decision of every controversy which may arise among its members. It is one of the great duties of government, one of the great objects for which it is instituted. Agents for the performance of this duty must be furnished, or the government fails in one of the great ends of its creation.

To whom more safely than to the judges are judicial questions to be referred? They are selected from the great body of the people for the purpose of deciding them. To secure impartiality, they are made perfectly independent. They have no personal interest in aggrandizing the legislative power. Their paramount interest is the public prosperity, in which is involved their own and that of their families.—*No* tribunal can be less liable to be swayed by unworthy motives from a conscientious performance of duty. It is not then the party sitting in his own cause. It is the application to individuals by one department of the acts of another department of the government. The people are the authors of all; the departments are their agents; and if the judge be personally disinterested, he is as exempt from any political interest that might influence his opinion, as imperfect human institutions can make him.

To the demand that the words which give the jurisdiction should be stated, I answer—they have already been stated.—The jurisdiction is expressly given in the words "the judicial power shall extend to all cases arising under this constitution." How does Hampden elude this provision? Not by denying that the case "arises under the constitution." That, not even he can venture to deny. How then does he elude it? He says that "these words may be otherwise abundantly satisfied."—But how "otherwise satisfied," he has not told us; nor can he. I admit there are other cases arising under the constitution. But the words are "all cases" and I deny that the word "some" can be substituted for "all," or that the word "all," can be satisfied if any one case can be withdrawn from the jurisdiction of the court. But the same reason may be assigned for withdrawing any or every other case. As each occurs, Hampden may say "these words may be otherwise abundantly satisfied." What peculiar reason has he assigned for this case which is not equally applicable to any and every other? His reason is that the case involves an enquiry, into the extent of the powers of the general government, and of a state government. And I ask what case can arise under the constitution which does not involve one or both of these enquiries? Let Hampden, if he can, state the case.

These words then cannot be otherwise satisfied. Hampden does not merely contract, he annihilates them.

But suppose him to succeed in excluding from the federal courts, all cases in which a question respecting the powers of the government of the union, or of a state can arise, are they to remain for ever undecided? Hampden does not say so. They must of course be decided in the state courts. He quotes, as sustaining his principles, a decision of the court of appeals in Virginia overruling an act of congress; and a decision of the supreme court of Pennsylvania (though in this he is mistaken) to the same effect. It follows then that great national questions are to be decided, not by the tribunal created for their decision by the people of the United States, but by the tribunal created by the state which contests the validity of the act of congress, or asserts the validity of its own act. Thus, in the language of the Federalist (No. 45), presenting to the world "for the first time, a system of government founded on an inversion of the fundamental principles of all government;"—"the authority of the whole society every where subordinate to the authority of the parts;"—"a monster in which the head is under the direction of the members."

Hampden is not more fortunate in the second principle with which he attempts to sustain this strange construction of the constitution, although he is pleased to term it "conclusive." "The rank of this controversy," he says, "between the head and one of the members of the confederacy, may be said to be superior to those depending between two of the members; and the lawyers well know that a specification beginning with a person or thing of an inferior grade, excludes those of a superior."

If I could be surprized at any argument found in the essays of Hampden, I should be surprized at this.

The jurisdiction of the federal courts, as described in the constitution, is dependent on two distinct considerations. The first is the character of the cause; the second, the character of the parties. All cases arising under the constitution, laws, and treaties of the

United States; all cases affecting public ministers; and all cases of admiralty and maritime jurisdiction; are cognizable in those courts, whoever may be the parties. The cases of the second class depend entirely on the character of the parties, without regard to the nature of the cause. It is not necessary that these two properties should be combined in the same cause, in order to give the court jurisdiction. If a case arise under the constitution, it is immaterial who are the parties; and if an alien be a party, it is not requisite that the case should arise under the constitution.

But McCullough, not the United States, is the party on the record; and were it otherwise, that circumstance would bring the case within, not exclude it from, the jurisdiction of the court. The constitution expressly gives jurisdiction to the courts of the union in "cases to which the United States shall be a party."

There is then no one objection made to the opinion of the supreme court which fails more entirely than this to its jurisdiction.

I have been induced to review these essays the more in detail, because they are intended to produce a very serious effect; and because they advance principles which go, in my judgment, to the utter subversion of the constitution. Let Hampden succeed, and that instrument will be radically changed. The government of the whole will be prostrated at the feet of its members; and that grand effort of wisdom, virtue, and patriotism, which produced it, will be totally defeated.

July 15, 1819   A FRIEND OF THE CONSTITUTION